To: Anne,

Love,

Jay Redmond

Mustard Seeds and Mountains: Battling the Beast Within

Mustard Seeds and Mountains: Battling the Beast Within

Joy Redmond

Joy Redmond

This is a work of non-fiction but some names have been changed or reduced to initials for their privacy.

ISBN: 9781073586684

"Truly I say to you, if you have faith the size of a mustard seed, you will say to this mountain, 'Move from here to there' and it will move, and nothing will be impossible to you." - Matthew 17:20

Preface

This is my personal story about my battle with cancer. I'm going to tell readers a few things about my life as far back as I can remember, and things I have been told by family. I'm doing this so the reader will get to know my personality and the things I have endured before cancer invaded my body. I'll tell readers about the tools, or recipe as I sometimes call it, that got me through my hard battle. This book isn't meant to be preachy. It isn't meant to try to force my beliefs on anybody. It isn't meant to change a reader's mind about what they believe or don't believe. I merely want to share what has worked for me. My reason for writing this book is to inspire, give hope, and instill the importance of never giving up.

Take what you want and leave the rest.

Chapter One

Nowadays, it's believed that a fetus can feel the mother's emotions and a fetus can hear voices. If this is true, then I learned to pray in the womb. My mother was a devout Christian and she was in church every Sunday morning and evening, and she attended prayer meetings every Wednesday night. As a fetus I heard her pray, I heard the prayers of the congregation, and I heard the beautiful hymns. To this day I love the old hymns that were sung back in my younger years.

If a fetus can hear voices, then I also learned to cuss while I was in the womb. My daddy was a drunken sailor and he spewed cuss words with every sentence he uttered. He was a nonbeliever and said that God, church, and all religious things were nothing but horse shit.

I was three years old and Mama was walking home from church, which was only a few blocks from the old shack we lived in. The house had three small rooms and seemed to be standing by sheer will. Mama had us children in tow. My oldest brother, Terril, was walking a few steps ahead of her. She was holding my hand, and carrying my youngest brother, Gary, in her arms.

I broke loose from her hand, ran toward the house, bounded the rickety steps, ran across the lop-sided porch, turned the door knob and it opened faster than I was expecting. I fell face down on the front room floor.

Daddy was sitting in the old wingback rocker, reading the newspaper. He loved the comic section. He dropped the paper, laughed and said, "Well, Punkin, did that communion wine get you drunk?" Punkin was Daddy's nickname for me, but the day I was born, he named me Carmeleta. I hated that name and I still do to this day.

I giggled as I got up and said, "Nah. Mama said it's grape juice. It ain't wine." Daddy dropped the paper to the floor and patted his legs, letting me know he wanted me to climb onto his lap. I ran to him and he lifted me onto his lap and wrapped his strong arms around me. Daddy holding me was the most wonderful feeling in the world. I never wanted Daddy to get far away from me when he was home.

Daddy hugged me and asked, "How was Sunday School and church?"

I giggled, and said, "It was horse shit."

Daddy threw back his head and laughed so hard my body was bouncing. Mama walked over to me, and I could almost see fire shooting from her eyes as she wagged her finger and said, "Young lady, if I ever hear you say that again I will spank you harder than you've ever been spanked!"

Mama's fussing and wagging her finger in my face made Daddy laugh harder. So, I laughed with him. I knew as long as I was in Daddy's arms, he wouldn't let Mama spank me. However, I was confused. I had said what I'd heard Daddy say many times. He was laughing and Mama was mad. It didn't make sense. I always sided with Daddy. If he said something, it was the gospel truth to me. Mama seemed to fuss at everything Daddy said and did, so I didn't pay any attention to her.

I was a daddy's girl. Anytime he was sitting, I was in his lap. When he was walking around I would hang on to his leg or hold his hand. Many times he carried me in his arms. I vividly remember him carrying me as we walked a few blocks to the corner liquor store so he could buy a pint. Mama would get mad and fuss and forbid him from taking me with him to a store of sin, as she called it.

I loved it when Daddy carried me to the sin store. Everybody in the store talked with me, played with me, and some would give me a piece of hard candy. Daddy always told me not to tell Terril that I got a piece of candy because he'd cry.

Terril always sided with Mama and believed that Daddy was hell bound. I didn't see anything wrong with Daddy buying himself something to drink. When Daddy tipped the pint to his lips, Terril became sullen and wouldn't talk to Daddy or me. I thought he was stupid. My Daddy was the greatest person on earth. He owned my heart and he could do no wrong in my eyes.

One Sunday, I woke up with a fever and a bad cough. Mama told me to stay home with Daddy. I was happy to be sick if it meant I could stay home and sit in Daddy's lap. I climbed into his lap and he wrapped one of his strong arms around me as he read the paper. "Well, Punkin, you won't have to listen to that damn preacher going on and on about hellfire and the smell of brimstone."

I knew what hellfire was because Preacher had imprinted a picture in my mind. I had no idea what brimstone was but I figured it was a horrible stink, like a skunk.

I dozed off and began to dream. I was digging my fingertips into a splintered, wooden plank and looking down on people. I could see them writhing in pain as flames encircled their bodies, and I could hear them crying in agony. I woke up screaming, "God, don't let me fall into hell! I've been a good girl."

Daddy patted my leg. "You're not going to hell. Goshdammit! I'm about ready to forbid your mama to ever take you back to church. That damn preacher is trying to scare his flock into believing what he does. And it won't take much more before I punch his lights out! Scaring a child is a sin, if ya ask me. Damn him to his hell!"

"But Daddy, Mama says he preaches straight from the Bible, and everything in the Bible is the truth."

"It might be Preacher's truth and your mama's truth, but that doesn't mean it *is* the truth. Someday, you'll make up your own mind as to what *you* believe. That's all I'm going to say about it right now. Go back to sleep."

Gary still slept in a crib. Some days, he'd be fussy while Mama was busy doing laundry, which she did on a scrub board. Sometimes her knuckles would bleed after she had scrubbed clothes for hours. I'd do my best to make Gary happy. I'd slip my hand through the slats of the crib, hold his tiny hand and tell him the story about the birth of Jesus. I was fascinated by the story of how Jesus was born in a stable and he slept in a manger.

I liked going to Sunday school. I enjoyed hearing the Bible stories, and I thought it was amazing how Noah put all the animals on the ark and they floated around and finally the ark came to rest on top of a mountain. When Sunday school was over and it was time for me to sit by Mama during church, I hated it. I couldn't sit still and I didn't want to hear anything the preacher said, especially when he started talking about hell. He described hell as a big lake of fire and the devil would gig you in the belly with a pitchfork and throw you in and you would burn forever. In my mind's eye I could see people in a lake of fire, burning, screaming, trying to find a way out and there was no way of escaping. It terrified me.

The preacher had a list of sins that would send you to hell: Drinking liquor, smoking, cussing, dancing, and the list went on and on. Everything he mentioned was what Daddy did. He drank, smoked, cussed, and he danced with me on Saturday nights when we listened to music on the old radio. I loved the Grand Ole Opry. Daddy was the greatest and I just wouldn't believe he was going to hell, yet I wasn't sure, because Mama said the preacher was right. So there were times when I was terrified that I would end up in hell with Daddy, because I planned on being just like him when I grew up.

I did my best to block Preacher's words out of my mind. I squirmed around in the pew, stood up, turned around and made faces at the people who were sitting behind us, and Mama would pinch my legs and tell me to sit down, sit still, and stop acting like a heathen. Many times, I stepped on people's toes as I tried to make my way past them to get away from Mama.

One harsh look from Mama made the people catch me and send me back to sit beside her. In my head I was saying, *Daddy is right. This is all horse shit.* I couldn't wait for the last hymn to be sung and the last prayer to be said so I could get home to Daddy and sit in his lap.

I'd learned not to talk about church or anything Preacher said when I was around Daddy. I was scared that Daddy would punch his lights out. I knew if he did, then Mama would be mad and she'd cry. I saw Mama cry a lot, and I knew it was because Daddy was a nonbeliever. I'd also overheard many talks between Mama and Grandmother about Daddy being a sinner and being hell bound, which made me mad, but also scared me.

Chapter Two

The summer before I turned four, Daddy moved us from Henderson, Kentucky, twenty miles out in the country, and three miles from the little community of Anthoston, Kentucky. Anthoston was what Daddy called a greasy spot in the road. It had a grocery store with gas tanks in front of it. One pump had regular gas and the other had Ethel. Daddy pulled up to the gas tanks. A man came out and asked Daddy what he wanted. Daddy said, "Do you have Ethel in that tank?" pointing to it.

The man said, "Yeah. Do ya want Ethel?"

Daddy said, "No, I want regular, but if Ethel is in that tank you better let her out before she drowns."

I laughed as I pictured Ethel trying to swim to the top of the tank. However, the man saw nothing funny about it. "How much do ya want?"

"A dollar's worth," Daddy answered. I don't remember Daddy ever buying more than a dollar's worth. There was also a small candy store a few yards up the road from the grocery. Every time we passed it, my mouth salivated for the taste of chocolate.

Daddy had rented a shotgun house that sat atop a high hill. The lane up to the house had gravel, but it also had large holes and Daddy did his best to dodge them. A few times a tire would fall into one. Daddy would get out of the car and push until the tire would roll over the hole, and I could hear him cussing with every heave. I laughed, and Mama would wag her finger in my face, which made me laugh harder.

When Daddy cussed, Terril would become sullen and tears would roll down his face. In my heart I knew he was crying because he believed that Daddy was going to hell. Gary laughed anytime I did, but Mama ignored him.

The three-room shotgun house was much larger than what we were used to in the three-room shack that we had lived in, in Henderson. Family members gave us more furniture and the best part was we all had beds. When we lived in town, Terril and I had to sleep on pallets in the front room. In the summer time, Mama fixed our pallets by the opened front window and we could feel a breeze. During winter, Mama put our pallets close to the pot-belly stove.

In our new home, the middle room was large enough for a double size bed for Terril and Gary. Granddaddy and Grandmother bought them a bed, which had a comfortable, soft mattress. They bought me a roll-away bed, which Daddy placed in the front room, just a few feet from his and Mama's bed. I loved the feel of the cozy mattress, but the best part was being close to Mama and Daddy.

I loved the wide open spaces where I could run barefoot. I loved to feel the grass between my toes. There was a well in the back yard. It was fun to stand

beside Daddy as he lowered a bucket that was attached to a long rope into the well. I giggled when I
heard the bucket hit the water. Daddy let me help
him pull the rope back to the top when the bucket
was full. There was a water dipper that hung on a
nail in the well frame. He'd dunk the dipper and hold
it to my lips. It was the best water in the world. I
didn't like the taste of the water in town. I was a happy child with all the better things we had by living in
the country.

Daddy planted a garden and we had fresh vegetables during the summer. Mama canned vegetables
for us to eat during the winter. The old house had a
front porch and Daddy hung a bench swing. Daddy
and I spent a lot of time on the swing and he'd tell his
tale tales and I'd laugh. I knew that most of the tales
he told weren't the whole truth, because I'd already
figured out that Daddy embellished everything he
said, and that's why Grandmother called him a big fat
liar. It didn't matter to me if his tales were real or lies,
I loved to hear them. Life just couldn't get any better
in my opinion.

By late fall, I noticed that Mama looked fat. Mama
had always been rail thin. I figured she got fat because we had plenty of food from the garden. When
we lived in town I'd overheard many conversations
between Mama and Daddy. Mama was always worried about money, and she'd fuss and tell Daddy that
we'd have more food if he didn't spend half his

paycheck on whiskey. Daddy still drank whiskey, but the food was free. It just sprouted out of the ground and Daddy didn't have to pay for it. It was amazing to me. It reminded me of the Bible story when God made it rain manna from heaven. Whatever manna was. I picture it as some kind of bread, maybe biscuits.

In early November, Daddy put up an old potbelly stove in the front room, not far from my roll-a-way. The heat felt wonderful. The old house had cracks in the walls, letting in cold air that made me shiver. When it rained with a hard wind behind it, rain also came through the cracks. Daddy would stuff the walls with rags and it helped, some.

One night, Mama put me to bed, pulled the covers up around my chin and I was nestled for the night. I always said a prayer with Mama before I went to sleep. We said the prayer that most children were taught back in my time.

"Now I lay me down to sleep
I pray the Lord my soul to keep
If I should die before I wake
I pray thee Lord, my soul to take."

"Mama, am I going to die before I wake up?"

"We never know when we're going to die. That's why we always have to be ready."

"How do I get ready?"

"By living a life that God teaches us in the Bible, and asking forgiveness for our sins."

"Like drinking whisky, smoking cigarettes, and cussing like Daddy does?"

"Well, yes, but there are many more sins we have to avoid."

"Like what?"

"We'll talk about it later. Just go to sleep. Please." Mama suddenly stopped talking and grabbed her fat stomach and moaned slightly.

"What's wrong, Mama?" I asked in a frantic voice.

"Nothing is wrong, honey, but you need to go to sleep. In the morning, you'll get a big surprise."

"Is Santa Clause coming?"

"No. Doctor Clay is coming. He's going to bring you a little brother or sister, but he won't come unless you go to sleep."

"Oh, wow. I sure hope I get a sister. I've got enough brothers."

The next morning I sat up in bed. I glanced straight ahead and saw Mama holding a baby, and she put it to her breast. I jumped out of bed and headed across the floor.

Mama said, "Hold it right there. You have to get dressed."

I wanted to cuss. Why did I have to get dressed before I could jump into bed beside her and see my little sister? I pulled my petticoat over my head, then

19

pulled my dress over my head. I ran across the cold floor, barefoot, and jumped into bed beside Mama. "What kind is it? Can I see it? Can I hold it?"

"You have a baby brother. Let Mama feed him, then you can hold him."

I was a bit disappointed that I didn't get a sister, but he looked so sweet, it didn't matter. I rubbed his tiny head as he suckled. "Mama, he has blond hair. That means he's an angel."

"He's our little angel. Daddy and I named him Dale. I have no idea where the blond hair comes from, but it'll probably turn dark as he gets older."

I thought it took forever for Dale to finish suckling and I was squirming, anxious to hold him. Finally, Mama said, "I think he's full for now." She laid him in my arms. My heart melted. He was the most precious baby in the world. From that moment on, he was *my* baby. He owned my heart.

As I held Dale and rubbed his head, I said, "Where's Daddy? Does he know we've got a new baby?"

"Daddy's on the front porch, smoking. He wanted to get outside. It was a long, hard night for him."

I stayed propped up in bed and held Dale until he was sound asleep. I laid him down, then put on my shoes and socks, not bothering to put on my coat and went outside to be with Daddy. He took a long drag from a cigarette, then he tipped a pint to his lips. Before I could say anything, I heard the snorting of mules and I saw their heads as they topped the hill. "It's Grandmother and Granddaddy!"

Daddy tossed the cigarette into the yard and stomped his foot. "I should have known those Bible-thumping turds would show up! Ol' Ive and Zada never miss a chance to ruin my day."

"But, Daddy, they probably brought us something. They always pack the wagon with stuff for us. Why don't you like them?"

"For lots of reasons, Punkin. As far as I'm concerned, ol' Zada is a leaping lizard from hell!"

As usual when Daddy made a statement, my mind's eye could see things. In my head I pictured a huge lizard with Grandmother's head attached and she was leaping from hell. I giggled. But when I saw the anger in Daddy's eyes, I stopped laughing. He was going to do something mean. I knew the look. I ran back inside yelling, "Grandmother and Granddaddy are here!"

Daddy came in behind me. "Punkin, get your coat. I'm going to Anthoston. I need gas for the car and I need to air up the tires. I don't know how much longer that old Model T is going to last, but I can't afford another one. It's all I can do to feed and clothe four kids. But I've got enough change for you to buy some candy if you wanna go with me."

"I wanna go! I can see Grandmother and Granddaddy when we come back home."

The smile on Mama's face let me know she was happy because her parents were there. "I'm going to the store with Daddy. He said I can buy some candy!" I proudly announced.

Terril eased his way to Daddy's side. "Can I go with you? I want some candy, too."

"Sure, son. Get your coat on and hurry. We'll go out the back door. I'm in no mood to face Ive and Zada."

With Daddy's help we quickly slipped on our coats that were hanging on a nail in the wall in the front room. We ran through the house, past Gary, who was sitting at the kitchen table, eating a cracker. Daddy hurried us out the back door, across the porch, down the rickety steps, and we jumped into the car.

Daddy started the car and we were headed down the steep hill before Grandmother and Granddaddy had the mules tied to the elm tree in the front yard. We waved at them. Daddy drove like a madman and cussed all the way to Anthoston.

I won't tell the story of what happened to me in the candy store. That story has been written in my book, 'Give Me Wings'. I wrote the book as fiction, for many reasons, but it's the story of my childhood. That day was when my personal angel, who I called Purple Angel, appeared to me. The angel had beautiful, silky purple wings. She came to me and she flew me to a special place in another dimension. Without

Purple Angel, I'm not sure I would have been able to mentally survive that day.

Purple Angel continued to appear to me during any crisis or heartbreak until I was twelve years old. As an adult, there are times when I feel her, but I never see her. My heart knows she's still with me and she always will be. I often pray to her.

pet. I loved being her pet. When it was picture day, Miss Sue combed my hair and she pinned a big white bow on the side. I thought I was beautiful. I disliked ng the bus, going to school, and seeing Miss Genevieve ... day, but I was also happy when school was out for summer break. I wanted to run barefoot and feel the grass between my toes, with the exception of stepping on a few hot gophers.

That summer I once hated chores at all and my best ... make Suzy once, but Teresa told Daddy I was not. And Teresa ruined my ... and I threw a mud pie at him.

I was ... happy child. ... was poor and we didn't ... much, but we were a family. We had each other and we had love. That's ... changed ... ... noticed as the summer wore on and Daddy became more moody, with Mama and the boys. He was even home a times a few times. Daddy had always treated me as if I was his princess, and he laughed at every thing I said. My heart ... like it broke in half when he yelled at me. The worst part was watching Mama cry. She cried every day. When I tried to comfort her, she'd tell me to leave her alone. They also broke my heart. My whole world was crumbling, and I had no idea how to fix it.

In mid-August, Daddy came home late from work one day. I was sitting on the bench swing, on the porch and waiting for him. I always sat beside him when he came home. My face lit up when I asked

Chapter Three

There was only one church in the small community of Anthoston, two miles from our house. Baptist wasn't Mama's religion, but she said it was a church and we'd attend every Sunday. I liked the preacher better than the one I'd had to listen to when we lived in town. He wasn't all about hellfire and brimstone, but he did preach about the same sins and hell.

To me it seemed that everything a person did or said was going to send them to hell. More and more I started to believe Daddy. It was all horse shit.

Daddy drove us to church and picked us up afterward. Every Sunday, Mama would beg Daddy to go inside with us. Daddy would cuss and tell her that hell would freeze over before he'd step foot inside a church. I always saw tears as Mama quickly wiped her eyes. She would never say anything to Daddy, she just ushered us children into church as fast as she could.

We had been living in the county for two years and I'd watch Terril run down the hill and get on the big, yellow school bus. I was so excited when September arrived and I'd get to ride the bus. I was finally a big girl and I'd be in first grade.

I loved my teacher, Miss Sue Robarts. She took a special interest in me and I was called the teacher's pet. I loved being her pet. When it was picture day, Miss Sue combed my hair and she pinned a big, white bow on the side. I thought I was beautiful. I liked riding the bus, going to school, and seeing Miss Sue every day, but I was also happy when school was out for summer break. I wanted to run barefoot and feel the grass between my toes with the exception of stepping on a few honeybees.

That summer I made mud pies, and I did my best to make Gary eat one, but Terril told Gary it was poison. Terril ruined my fun and I threw a mud pie at him.

I was a happy child. We were poor and we didn't have much, but we were a family, we had each other and we had love. To me that made us rich. However, I noticed as the summer went on that Daddy became more cross with Mama and the boys. He was even cross with me a few times. Daddy had always treated me as if I was his princess, and he laughed at everything I did or said. My heart felt like it broke in half when he yelled at me. The worst part was watching Mama cry. She cried every day. When I tried to comfort her, she'd tell me to leave her alone. That also broke my heart. My whole world was crumbling and I had no idea how to fix it.

In mid-August, Daddy came home late from work one day. I was sitting on the bench swing, squirming and waiting for him. He always sat beside me when he came home. My face lit up when I heard the old car with the busted tailpipe coming up the hill. It was 'Daddy-and-me' time. As Daddy walked across the yard, I noticed his head was tucked and he didn't have the lively step he usually did. Shivers ran up my spine. Something bad had happened, I just knew it, and whatever it was, it was going to make Mama cry. My heart was beating so fast I could barely breathe as he made his way up the lopsided steps and walked across the porch.

"Daddy, are you gonna sit beside me? I want you to tell me some stories."

Daddy blew a hard breath, wiped his hand across his face and his weary steps told me I was right. Whatever he was going to say, wasn't going to be good. I didn't say a word as he sat down on the swing beside me. I slipped my hand into his and waited.

Finally, he told me he was moving to Indianapolis, Indiana, where he had a job that paid good money. He said the shipyard in Evansville, Indiana, where he was a welder had closed down. He said he was out of a job unless he went to Indianapolis, and he had to go because it was the only way he could make a living. He explained that Indianapolis was a long way from where we lived and he wouldn't see us very often.

I refused to believe what he was saying. There was no way Daddy would move off and leave me. He just couldn't. I'd die if he did.

However, Daddy did leave us that evening. I watched him load his old car while tears blinded me. He didn't even kiss me goodbye, he just got in the car and drove down the steep hill as if he was going to the gas station and would be back soon. I stood and waved as I watched the car disappear. I pinched my leg as hard as I could. I thought I was having a nightmare and I wanted to wake up. But the pain I inflicted told me I was awake and Daddy had abandoned me. My heart felt as if it had broken into a million pieces and there was no way it would ever mend.

I sat down on the top step in deep thought. If Daddy left me, that meant he didn't love me. If Daddy didn't love me that meant I was unlovable. I wasn't worth a dime. I cried until I couldn't shed any more tears. Then I got mad. I stood up, placed my hands on my hips and said, "James Edward Littrell, you're a big fat liar, just like Grandmother said. You could have found another job in Evansville if you'd tried. You just don't love any of us and you wanted to leave. I hate you!" Though words of hate came out of my mouth, my heart was crying, *I love you with all my heart. I'll love you until the day I die. I can't live without you.*

After Daddy left we were stuck out in the country with no transportation and no source of income. Daddy had promised Mama he would send her money by Western Union every payday. Sometimes, Uncle Tubby and Aunt Loretta would come get us and take us to Henderson so Mama could check with Western Union. And sometimes Uncle Lloyd came for us. Daddy sent little money, and a few times he sent nothing. When none of the family could come get us and take us to Henderson, Mama would walk us children three miles into Anthoston. The Greyhound bus made a daily run on Highway 41. Mama would flag down the bus and we'd ride to town. If there was money for us at Western Union, Mama would go to the Red Front and buy the cheapest items she could find, hoping it would be enough to keep us fed until Daddy sent more. But it never did.

Winter arrived and soon all the canned food was gone, and the coal house was empty. When the last morsel of food had been eaten, Mama would sit in the old wingback rocker, gather us children around her and tell us to pray. Within a few hours, a neighbor or a member of the church would bring us groceries. When the last lump of coal had been burned and we were freezing, Mama would put all four of us children in her bed and pile all the blankets we had on top of us. She told us to pray. Within a few hours, coal would be delivered. One time we were in the middle of praying for coal and before we could say amen, we heard the roaring of a Russell Wilson Coal truck coming up the steep hill.

I began to believe in prayer with all my soul. I knew Mama was right, and Daddy was the one who was full of horse shit.

These are all the details I'm going into about my family almost starving and freezing, as I've already told it in my book 'Give Me Wings'. I'll move on to the most devastating day of my life, but with little details. They are also in 'Give Me Wings'. I feel it's important to tell this part so I can piece together the rest of my life for a reader.

Every day, I was complaining of headaches, and my eyes watered when I tried to read my primer, and the words blurred. Mama said she'd get me to an eye doctor as soon as possible. It had been a while since any family member had come out to the country to give us a ride to town.

January 4th, 1951, we walked to Anthoston so Mama could flag down the Greyhound. Mama left Terril and Gary with a church member who lived in Anthoston. She took Dale with her because he was only four years old, and he cried when Mama left him.

We flagged down the Greyhound and twenty minutes later we were at the bus station in Henderson. The eye doctor's office was only a few blocks away. The doctor examined my eyes and determined there was nothing wrong with my sight. He thought it was allergies and he gave Mama a bottle of drops and told her to put two drops in my eyes twice a day. After we left the doctor's office we had a few hours before the Greyhound was ready to make the run back toward Anthoston.

Mamaw and Papaw lived across town from the doctor's office, but Mama said the sun was shining and if we walked fast, we wouldn't get too cold. I was always happy to see Mamaw. She'd hug me, hold me in her lap, and like Daddy, she was full of tall tales that made me laugh. Mamaw always had plenty of food cooked. That day she had banana pudding, my favorite. Our stomachs were filled that day. Dale and I played hide-and-go-seek while Mama talked to Mamaw.

Later that day, Mama called us and told us to get our coats because it was time for us to walk back to the bus station. She said the bus would be ready to roll by the time we got there. I never wanted to leave Mamaw, but I hoped I'd see her again soon. We walked back to the bus station as it was getting dark.

By the time the Greyhound reached the intersection of Highway 41 and Frog Island Road, it was pitch dark. We walked down the steps of the Greyhound, Mama holding Dale's hand in her right hand, and mine in her left. We walked behind the bus and started across the road.

A speeding car was blinded by the bright bus lights, and Mama didn't see the lights of the oncoming car. The car struck us, hitting Dale first, then Mama, then me. I was thrown 150 feet and landed in a deep ditch of mud. Mama and Dale were killed. I spent several months in the hospital.

After my release, Aunt Loretta took me home with her and kept me until the cast that went from my waist, down both legs to the tips of my toes was ready to be removed. I had to learn to walk again. It was a struggle, but I finally mastered it.

The full story of this accident and my recovery is told in 'Give Me Wings'.

For the next two years I was in and out of seven homes and seven schools. When I was ten years old, I went to live with Thelma and Shelby Grossman, who were almost as old as my grandparents and they had no children. I thought the Grossmans were strange people and I didn't want to stay with them, but no family member was able to take me in.

After I had been living with the Grossmans for eight months, one day Thelma explained that she and Shelby were going to adopt me. She explained the process of adoption, which I didn't completely understand, but I plainly understood when she told me that Daddy would sign over all rights to me and I wouldn't be allowed to see him until I was eighteen. My heart felt as if it would explode and burst out of my body.

That night I prayed to die. I wanted go to heaven and be with Mama and Dale. I thought death was better than living with weird people and being forbidden to see Daddy until I was eighteen. The next morning when Thelma woke me up for breakfast, I was mad. Why didn't God take me to heaven?

When Daddy signed the adoption papers, again I hated him. First he abandoned me without glancing back, then he gave me away to strangers as if I were no more than a stray pup. A large part of me *did* die that day. I was no longer a Littrell. I was a Grossman. I was stripped of my identity. That was the day my personality split.

When I was at home I assumed the personality of Joyce, which was the new name they decided to give me. When I was away from my adopted parents, I assumed the personality of Carmeleta. At times when I was at home, I'd forget which personality was supposed to take the lead, and Carmeleta would pop out. Thelma would open a kitchen drawer, take out the butter paddle and I'd get a spanking.

See 'Give Me Wings' and 'Wings and Beyond' for the story of my life with the Grossmans.

The Grossmans were good parents in many ways, but they made my life miserable in more ways. By the time I was eighteen, I hated them. All I thought about day and night was how to escape. I thought of calling Daddy since I was of legal age, but he had remarried and he had five other children. Terril, Gary, and I had lived with Daddy and my stepmother for three months shortly after Mama and Dale were killed. My stepmother didn't like us and we hated her. The thought of living with her again was worse than the thought of going to hell.

The details of Terril, Gary, and I living with Daddy and my stepmother is in 'Give Me Wings'. It was truly mortal hell.

My only way to get away from my adopted parents was to marry the first guy who proposed to me. I met him at a Halloween party. We had only been on two dates when he asked me to marry him.

Hot damn! He was my way out, though he was virtually a stranger. It didn't matter. He lived in Owensboro, Kentucky, a town forty miles from Henderson. It was far enough away that I wouldn't have to see Thelma and Shelby every day, and I wouldn't get phone calls every day because there would be long-distance charges, I had learned that the Grossmans didn't spend a penny they didn't deem necessary. I figured Thelma would call once a week, and that was plenty for me. The wedding took place December 30th, 1960.

I was finally free. Or so I thought.

Chapter Four

I won't give the name of the man I married out of re-spect for his family. By marrying him to get away from the Grossmans, as the old saying goes, I had jumped out of the frying pan and into the fire. His mother, who I won't name, was the mother-in-law from hell. She completely dominated my life and my husband went along with her. I never said or did any-thing right according to the two of them. I wasn't worth a dime.

I had married a narcotics-using asshole and a wife beater. The only person he loved was himself. What he wanted or needed was all that mattered. What his wife and children needed didn't matter as long as he was happy. For seven years I packed black eyes and busted lips in ice. The only good thing that came from that marriage was my oldest daughter, Cathye, and my son, Scott.

I prayed every day, asking God to show me a way out of the marriage. I knew if I stayed with him, he would kill me, or I'd end up killing him. Finally, God opened a door, and I was free of him. It had been seven years of mortal hell.

Freedom at last. Or so I thought, again.

The details of this marriage are in my book "Wings and Beyond". It is also written as fiction, for many reasons, but it's the story of my young adult years.

I was twenty-five years old when the divorce was final. I thought I was an old woman and didn't think anybody would want to marry a woman my age with two children. I figured I was doomed to live my life single and rear my children the best I could.

I laugh now when I think back about how I was convinced I was an old woman when I turned twenty-five. I'm now seventy-six, and I dare anybody to call me old. I'm young at heart and in my mind I'm still twenty-five.

As I played with my grandchildren when they were school age, I was a little girl again, and I got the pleasure of living the childhood that I was robbed of. When they were teenagers, I had fun with them, and I was living my teen years that I was robbed of.

Age is just a number. Nothing more.

I struggled as a single mother trying to provide for two children, but with the help of my adopted parents, we made it. However, their help always came with strings attached and it was a tough pill to swallow. I swallowed hard, and kept going.

Two years after my divorce I met a man who fell in love with me at first sight. I wasn't in love with him, but I liked him. He was funny and kept me laughing. My two children were crazy about him. Two months after we started dating, he proposed. I was hesitant about marrying him, but I didn't think it was fair to rob my children of a daddy figure. Even before we married, they called him Daddy Steve. For their sake, I married him.

I knew he drank but I had no idea how much. Soon after I married him, I realized he was an alcoholic. For two years I threatened to leave him, but he'd cry and promise me he'd stop drinking. As with all alcoholics, it wasn't possible. I was making plans to get out of the marriage when I found out I was pregnant. The only good thing that came from that marriage was my youngest daughter, Michelle. After she was born, I didn't want my three children to come from a broken home. I did my best to stay in the marriage for my children's sake, even if it meant misery for me.

I kept praying, asking God to show me what I was supposed to do. The last year I spent with him, when I prayed for an answer, the little voices in my head (I call them angels talking to me) told me loud and clearly. "Divorce him. You're doing your children more harm than good. He's destroying their self-worth with his belligerent attitude toward them. And he's destroying yours too. You're in a toxic environment."

Once again I was beginning to feel that I wasn't worth a dime. After all, he was choosing a bottle over me and the children. At that time I didn't realize that alcoholism is a disease. He didn't choose the bottle over me and the children. The devil chose to use his disease to destroy him and his family. I know the difference now. And I totally forgive him.

We divorced in 1974, but we remained friends until he died in 2005. I cried my eyes out for my daughter. She had never had a daddy because of his drinking problem. But he sobered up the last five years of his life. She only had five short years to know what it was like to have a good daddy. She loved him and wanted him around to be a granddaddy to her oldest child, Julia. Julia never got the chance to know him.

The full details of this marriage are in 'Wings and Beyond'.

Here I was, again a single mother. I worked two jobs but we still couldn't survive, and I had little time to spend with my children. Michelle was only three years old. I hated being away from my baby. Once again my adopted parents came to my rescue and made sure we didn't go hungry and our needs were met.

A year after the divorce, my adopted parents, who I called Mother and Dad, bought me a house in a nice neighborhood. But their generosity came with strings attached as usual. I *would* live by their rules. If I stepped out of *their line* one time, then they threatened to cut me off and even cut me out of their will.

I'd been their daughter for twenty-two years, doing their bidding. I wasn't about to lose it all at this time in my life. So, once again I had to bow to them, which caused more resentment to grow inside me. I was grateful for all they did and I always will be, but the price I had to pay made it hard to be grateful at times. I've never been a person who takes to dictation and goes by other's rules. I never will be. For the sake of my children I put up with it at the time, but I swore to myself that the day would come when I wouldn't.

My day finally arrived. I sold my house, packed up my belongings, my children, and moved to Cape Girardeau, Missouri, May 25th, 1976.

I knew the move would be the thing that would get me cut out of my parents will, and I would receive no help from them in any way. I was on my own. I had faith that God would show me a way.

Freedom at last. Or so I thought, once more.

tramp and I'm proud of it. I'd rather be a tramp than live in the eighteenth century that you are stuck in."

Mother let the waterworks flow, but I ignored her. I was expecting Dad to let go with his temper, but all he did was shake his head. I think he knew he wouldn't have any children. Either that, or he had finally learned it did no good to say anything to my hardheaded ingrate of a daughter.

Mother also interrogated my children, which infuriated me. However, as young as they were, they knew not to answer her. They merely shrugged their shoulders and said, "I don't know."

We were happy in Cave. It was a small town and the people were nice and friendly. We spent two good years there. The winters of 1977 and 78 were more brutal than I could stand. I promised myself if the sun ever did shine again and if the snow ever melted, I'd move to Florida. I'd had plenty of snow and ice that I wanted for a lifetime. I never wanted to see another snowflake as long as I lived.

The whole story of our two years in Missouri is in my book "Village and Beyond".

July 1979, I sold my house, and we moved to Clearwater, Florida. We were far enough away that my parents couldn't visit for a little while, which was a great relief. However, they did make the trip down the week before each Christmas, and the week

Chapter Five

To my great surprise, the move didn't get me cut out of the will, and there was no threat about them not helping me financially. However, Mother demanded that I write a letter every week, and she did the same. In each letter she wrote she asked at least fifty questions. I did my best to answer with a lie that I thought she'd believe. I wasn't living the lifestyle she and Dad had always demanded, so lies were necessary to satisfy them. If I should fail to answer one question, then I got a phone call. I could always think quickly, and I'd come up with something that she seemed to buy.

The only bad thing about moving was I was still close enough for a monthly visit from my parents. Each time they came, Mother would do a search of every room in the house. She opened my dresser and chest of drawers and picked up each item, making sure nothing was hidden, and she went through my closet. I knew that she was making sure there was no evidence that I might have had an overnight male visitor. More resentment grew inside me and was quickly turning into hate. I found my emotions, but I couldn't stop them. Mother always said my wardrobe was trampish. I tried to hold my tongue but I couldn't. My anger jumped out of my mouth. "I'm a tramp and I'm proud of it. I'd rather be a tramp than live in the eighteenth century that you are stuck in!"

Mother let the waterworks flow, but I ignored her. I was expecting Dad to let go with his temper, but all he did was shake his head. I think he did it so he wouldn't scare my children. Either that or he had finally learned it did no good to say anything to me, his hardheaded tramp of a daughter.

Mother also interrogated my children, which infuriated me. However, as young as they were they knew not to answer her. They merely shrugged their shoulders and said, "I don't know."

We were happy in Cape. It was a small town and the people were nice and friendly. We spent two great years there. The winters of 1977 and 78 were more brutal than I could stand. I promised myself if the sun ever did shine again and if the snow ever melted, I'd move to Florida. I'd had all the cold, snow and ice that I wanted for a lifetime. I never wanted to see another snowflake as long as I lived.

The whole story of our two years in Missouri is in my book 'Wings and Beyond'.

July 1978, I sold my house and we moved to Clearwater, Florida. We were far enough away that my parents couldn't come for monthly visits, which was a great relief. However, they did make the trip down the week before each Christmas, and the weekly letters were still required. So the dutiful letter writing continued.

We loved Florida. It was our paradise. After five years, my world fell apart again and I had no choice but to leave my beloved Florida.

The details of what happened are in my book 'Wings and Faith'.

I sold my house and rented a home from my brother, Terril, in Cleveland, Tennessee. We loved the mountains. The view from every window of the house was beauty surrounding us. Jobs were hard to find in the small town of Cleveland. I found a job, but I didn't make close to enough money to support us. By this time my oldest daughter had married and divorced and I had a two-year-old granddaughter, Chrissy. I took them in. More expenses, and there was no way for me to make ends meet.

Again, my adopted parents saved us by sending money. However, since Cleveland was only a five hour drive from Henderson, I was told I *would* make a monthly visit to see them. They were up in their 70's and the drive, especially through the mountains was too much for them.

I made my dutiful visits and the once a week letter writing continued. Resentment continued to grow in my soul.

I had been living in Cleveland for six months, loving every minute of the beauty, and the pleasure of being close to my brother, my niece and my nephew. We had many meals together, many laughs, and it was great being close to my blood family after so many years apart.

A man who had met me several years ago when I lived in Florida, and visited Gary who was stationed at Ft. Stewart, Georgia, showed up at my door. He had heard from Gary that I had moved to Cleveland, Tennessee. He was smitten with me, and he made trips to see me every weekend. He wined and dined me and said all the things a woman wants to hear.

After dating for a month, I fancied myself in love with him. He owned a motorcycle shop in Hinesville, Georgia, and made good money. He proposed, and I accepted. He lived in Midway, Georgia, in a beautiful house on Lake George. Not only was I in love, but I would be living in a house on a lake, something I'd always dreamed of.

By the time I married him and moved to Midway, my oldest daughter, Cathye was living with a man, and she and my granddaughter, Christina, had their own place. My son, Scott, had gone back to Owensboro, Kentucky to live with his grandparents when we moved from Florida. Michelle and I were the only two that made the move to Georgia.

For five years, I was in love with a man who I thought was the greatest man and husband on earth. I won't mention his name out of respect for his family. However, by our 5th anniversary, I was knocked to my knees when certain evidence began to appear and

I realized who he really was. By this time the motor-cycle shop had gone belly-up. He managed to sell the shop and inventory. We paid off a mountain of debt, but we still owed another mountain and we lost the house on Lake George.

We moved to Valdosta, Georgia, where my hus-band went to work for his daddy's insurance compa-ny. I went to work for a doctor's office. Even with two checks, we couldn't make ends meet and the bills were piling up.

Once again my world fell apart, but I had no way out for another two years. Mother passed away in 1985 and Dad wasn't as generous as she had been. He knew I was working and he thought my husband was providing well for me. I never told him about our fi-nancial situation. I was on my own. I took a second job and saved every dime I could until I had enough money to get away.

The complete details of that marriage are in my book, 'Wings and Faith'.

Michelle and I went to live with my brother, Ter-ril, and his wife Chloe, who had moved to Chatta-nooga, Tennessee. By this time my daughter, Cathye, had another little girl, Crystal. However, her relation-ship had fallen apart and she had moved back to Henderson. My son, Scott, was also the father of three children, Brandon, Ashley and Dorian. They lived in Evansville, Indiana, just ten miles across the bridge from Henderson. At age forty-six, I was a grand-mother of five.

Living in Chattanooga, I was closer to my oldest children and grandchildren. I used part of my savings for gas, and I visited them once a month. It was so wonderful to see and hold my five precious grand-babies. I cried all the way back to Chattanooga every time I had to kiss them goodbye.

I filled out applications at every hospital, clinic and doctor's office in Chattanooga. I was never called for an interview. My savings were dissolving with every passing day. I was frantic. I prayed with all my heart for God to help me find a job. It didn't happen.

Michelle took a job working at Ruby Falls, a week after we arrived in Chattanooga. It wasn't great pay, but she was able to make her car payments, pay her insurance, and buy her personal items.

After three months, Terril, a Methodist minister, was transferred to Bristol, Virginia. He and Chloe said we could go with them. We went to Bristol to check out the parsonage. It was barely big enough for two people. There was no way the four of us could live together.

There was only one thing for me to do. I called Dad and asked if Michelle and I could live with him until we found jobs and got a place of our own. He said, "No, I like living by myself. You've always hat-ed Henderson, so I see no reason for you to come back."

I was furious. I dropped the phone and said, "Well, thanks a lot, you old fart. I'm soon to be home-less and on the streets!"

Chloe had lunch ready by the time I was off the phone. I told everybody that Dad said I couldn't live with him, and nobody could believe their ears. I did my best to eat, but anger and hurt feelings had taken my appetite. I forced the last bite down, looked at Michelle and said, "Finish eating, then you and I are going to Henderson. I want him to tell me to my face. It's too easy to say no on the phone."

We made the trip, and as I suspected, Dad didn't have the nerve to say to my face that we couldn't stay with him. I hated the thought of coming back to Hen-derson more than I have words to express, but I had no choice.

Two weeks later, Michelle and I moved in with Dad. I pulled the car into the driveway and said, "It's May the twenty-fifth, exactly fifteen years to the very day that I left Henderson, swearing on everything ho-ly that I'd never return. Well, eat my words one more time. Here we are."

"Yep, here we are. And my daddy lives here, too. That makes me happy."

"That's good, honey. I want you to have a rela-tionship with your daddy. He's come for visits in eve-ry state we've lived in. He was his old silly, funny self when he came. I enjoyed his visits as much as you did. Here's hoping he has his drinking under control."

"Yeah, I sure hope so. He's hard to take when he's drinking. I learned that when I came to Henderson, for summer vacation."

I patted her leg. I had my doubts about his drinking, but I didn't want her to lose hope.

The only thing that held me together was being in the same town as my three children and my five grandchildren. Scott and his wife Beth had moved back to Henderson at this time.

The rest of this story is in my book, 'Wings and Faith'

Chapter Six

Michelle married in May, 1994. She married into a good family and I adored her husband. I was anxious to get another grandbaby. My fifth one was eleven years old. My arms ached to hold a newborn. After five years, Michelle said, "Mom, I don't guess it was meant for me to be a mother. I'll just settle for mothering my dogs. I love them like they were my children, anyway."

I was disappointed, but I accepted that I would only have five grandchildren.

January 1999, Michelle rushed into the house yelling, "Mom, you're never going to believe this, but—"

I finished her sentence. "You're pregnant!" I gave her a big hug, my heart overflowing with joy.

"How did you know? I wanted to surprise you."

"Mamas always know things. The glow on your face gave it away."

"It'll be here the last of October. I hope I have a boy. Marcus wants a boy so badly, and I don't want to disappoint him."

"I hope it's a little girl. And Marcus will be happy with her. Most all men want a son, but they're crazy about their little girls."

October 20th 1999, Michelle gave birth to my granddaughter, Julia. The minute I held her in my arms, she looked into my eyes and stole my heart forever. I was at a very low point in life, but this little bundle of joy gave me a new lease on life. She became the very air I breathed. She was the sunshine in my life on my darkest days. Julia gave me back my life, with a reason and purpose to go on. I felt happiness that had been missing for years.

I clung to Julia, a tiny mite, to get me through and sustain me when one crisis after another came with each day. My two oldest children and Dad had me on the verge of a complete breakdown, mentally and physically.

Dad died in April, 2003. He was three months shy of being ninety-six. It had been a hard twelve years living with him and being his caretaker. I was sad the day he died, but I was also relieved. I was finally out of Grossman bondage. I could be *me*. I no longer had to use two personalities.

After fifty years, Carmeleta was free.

I still go by the name Joyce, but Carmeleta is my personality. She's a joker, a prankster, and has the ability to laugh at any situation. Being able to laugh, joke, and find the funny side of every curve that life throws me, is how I've survived. I also love to mess with people's heads, especially the ones who have little to no personality. I can't stand to be around somber people, and I don't stop messing with them until I at least get a smile or a small chuckle.

Julia was still the sunshine of my days. When she was two years old, Michelle and Marcus decided they wanted to try for another baby. For the next ten years, I waited for the news that I was going to get my seventh grandbaby. It didn't happen.

When Julia was thirteen I received a phone call from her. She said, "Nana, Mama is pregnant and she's crying her eyes out. She said forty-one was too old to be a new mother. I don't know what to say to her."

"Put her on the phone, honey," I said, my heart doing a tap dance in my chest. My arms ached to hold a newborn. Michelle and I had a long conversation, and she felt better by the time we hung up the phone. I knew this baby that I call our miracle baby would be a great blessing.

March 20th, 2013, Olivia was born. I was seventy-plus and I wondered how I'd ever be able to keep up with her when she started walking, running, and getting into everything. She started walking a week before her first birthday. Two weeks later she was running as if she were a motor boat. But keep up with her I did, and it wasn't much of an effort. I've always been a ball of energy. Nothing could slow me down, let alone stop me.

She's been the greatest joy of my life for the past five years. I nicknamed her Tiny Terror. She's a hoot, and she has my personality. I'm not sure if that's good or bad, but I get a kick out of everything she says and does. In my eyes, she can do no wrong. Our relationship reminds me of Daddy and me. So many years ago.

All my life I have prayed. Sometimes it took God a few years, but my prayers were answered. I prayed with all my soul and even tried making a plea bargain with God, when I knew I had no choice but to return to Henderson. I laugh now as I remember my plea, I said, "God, I'll dig peanuts and live in a hovel if you won't send me back to Henderson." I soon learned He doesn't make plea bargains.

I've been living in Henderson for twenty-eight years now, and I've been shown one hundred thousand reasons *why* I *had* to come back. Amazing. God did answer my prayers by saying no to my pleas. I've finally learned to stop arguing with God. He always knows best, even if I don't think so at the time. Time has proven me wrong. Every time.

This is all the background of my life that I'm going to give in this book, but I want to add— a man who I will refer to as Nameless, because he's a private person and he wouldn't want his real name used, was my knight in shining armor when he paid me a visit two years after Dad Grossman died. I added this part because Nameless will be mentioned many times as I write about my battle with ovarian cancer. He is the same Nameless I refer to in my Facebook posts.

Chapter Seven

The rest of this book I will insert comments from notes that I wrote in a journal I started after I found out I had cancer. I'll also include comments that I've posted on Facebook. As I've said before, I'm a jokester and a prankster. I used my humor to keep me going every time I had to see a doctor or take chemo treatments. I know my humor, as warped as it is at times, is my defense mechanism, but it works for me.

The horrible thing about cancer is you can have it for years before you have any signs or symptoms. I have no idea how long the cancer had been growing in my body before I noticed I was losing my energy. I've always been able to go from morning to night and never stop. I didn't know the meaning of the word tired. At this time I just thought it was age and a case of 'I don't want to'. As the days went by, my 'I don't want to' was becoming a daily thing.

The second week in May, 2018, I came down with a head cold. When I have head colds I always use Zi-cam Nasal Spray. Within three days it knocks it out. This time it didn't work. I had congestion in my lungs and I was coughing. I bought a box of Alka-Seltzer Plus pills. I took the pills for a week. They didn't work. I knew I'd just have to wear it out. For two weeks I coughed so hard it felt as if I had pulled the muscles loose from my ribs. Then it just stopped.

A few days after my coughing spells were over I had severe pain in my bladder. It had been years since I'd had a bladder infection, but the pain wasn't like any that I'd had before. There was no pain when I peed, the flow was normal, and no pain after I peed. However, I went to my primary doctor. He did a urinalysis. It was clean. But to be on the safe side he put me on a round of Macrodantin. I took the pills, but got no relief. I went back to my family doctor.

I got a bit tired of being asked the same questions every time I went see my family doctor. The nurse would ask, "Do you use street drugs? Do you smoke? Do you drink alcohol?"

I said, "You ask me the same questions every time I come in here. My answers are in your computer."

She answered, "Yes, they are, but I'm required to ask them every time you come in."

That day I wasn't in the mood to go through all the same questions. When I want to be interrogated, I'll go to the police station.

When she asked, "Do you drink alcohol?"

I said, "If you're buying, I certainly do. Happy hour starts at five. Which bar do you have in mind?" She gave me a snide look, closed her computer and made a quick exit from the room. I just sat there and laughed.

Doctor R referred me to a neurologist. It took two weeks to get an appointment. By this time I was in unbearable bladder pain. And my abdomen was swelling more by the day. I thought I had coughed so hard that it caused my bladder to prolapse.

The next day, Michelle called and asked if I felt like keeping Olivia for a couple hours. She had shopping to do and Olivia wanted to stay with me. I told her to bring my baby to me. I'd crawl from my death bed to see and play with Olivia. Before Olivia arrived, I said to Nameless, "It's Tiny Terror day. We'll run and play and chase rabbits. I hope my bladder doesn't fall out. She'll think it's a ball and she'll be bouncing it around the yard. And she might decide to shoot a few hoops. This should be an interesting day."

I made it for two hours with her, but I was exhausted by the time Michelle picked her up. I couldn't believe how quickly I was losing strength. But I kept pushing. I never give in to anything.

The next day I had to make a quick run to the Dollar General Mart. I was holding my swollen belly up with both hands, trying to hurry across the parking lot. I got a few strange looks. So, I said, "What are you staring at? Haven't you ever seen a seventy-five-year-old pregnant woman before? I've got to hold this kid in until I buy some diapers and stuff. I'm due any day." Nobody had anything to say.

Finally, my appointment date arrived. I told Doctor B my symptoms. He said, "I know exactly what your problem is. You're seventy-five and your vagina is dry and sticking together because you have no hormones. But I'll do a vaginal exam and make sure your bladder isn't prolapsed."

"Well, if you know what my problem is I'll take your word for it. There's no reason for a vaginal exam."

"Yes, it's important. I might feel something that will tell me you might have another problem."

I undressed from the waist down and I thought, *"Well, shit!" Here I am on a table, my legs spread-eagle and a man will be sitting on a stool with a bird's-eye view. If that's not humiliating enough, he'll turn on what I call a spotlight. The overhead light is bright, and he'll have his face in my business, so why does he need a spotlight? More humiliation.*

The exam was painful. I gritted my teeth and I felt tears welling. It seemed to take him forever to feel around and I was tempted to squash his head between my knees. I said, "Take it easy, man. There hasn't been a train through that tunnel in years!"

"I'm glad I'm done. I'm laughing too hard to do my job," he said.

"Well, I'm glad I gave you a laugh. Is my bladder prolapsed or not?"

"No. Your bladder is intact." Still laughing, he left the room and told me to get dressed and he'd be back in a few minutes. He came back and said, "I'm going to give you a prescription for Premarin cream. Insert it once a day for five weeks and you'll be fine."

I stood up and said, "Look at my stomach," as I pulled up my blouse. "I was this size when I was five months pregnant. What's causing the swelling?"

"It's gravity. It happens. Use the cream and make an appointment to come back and see me in five weeks." Out the door he went.

I looked at the nurse and said, "Gravity, my ass. My abdomen has gone from a small pouch to the size of a five month fetus in one month!"

She sweetly said, "The swelling could be caused by the lack of hormones. He knows what he's talking about. He's a very good doctor."

I left the office thinking my problem had been found and soon I would be pain free. I used the Premarin for three weeks. No relief. I reminded myself that Doctor B had said five weeks, but my inner voice (I call it the angels talking to me) was saying I had been wrongly diagnosed.

Chapter Eight

By mid-June, I was getting weaker and I wanted to take a nap in the afternoons. I've never taken naps. There was always something I wanted to do. Naps were for babies, not me.

That night I was lying in bed, watching a movie when I felt something pop up in my left side about three to four inches from my belly-button. I pulled my pajama top up and I could see a golf ball sized knot. "What in the hell?" I mumbled. I massaged the knot and it seemed to go down. There was no pain, so I thought it might be a muscle spasm. However, the next morning it was still there and I could see it. I kept thinking it would go away.

The next three nights, more knots the same size popped up. I was beginning to panic. I knew my lack of hormones in my bladder wouldn't cause masses in my side. I stopped using the hormone cream.

I made an appointment with my primary doctor. He pushed on the masses, but there was no pain, which I was grateful for. When he finished with his exam, I stood up and said, "Do you see the swelling in my abdomen? I'm getting bigger by the day."

He said, "Yes, I see it. You're very swollen. I don't know why and I have no idea what the masses are, but you need to see a surgeon."

I didn't know a surgeon in this town. Doctor R gave me two names. I just picked one. He said he would send in a referral.

Finally, a doctor recognized abnormal swelling along with four masses, and he knew I had a serious problem. He didn't venture to say what it might be because it wasn't his field of medicine. However, I saw the look of concern on his face.

It took two weeks to get an appointment with Doctor T, the surgeon. The long waits to see doctors were grating on my nerves. Fear was gripping me and I was getting angry and irritable. It was a long two weeks.

I went to see Doctor T. He had the personality of a stick, but personality didn't matter if he could figure out my problem. I told him my symptoms. He pushed on the masses in my left side. By this time another one had popped up on the right side. He felt it, too.

He coldly said, "I'll order a CT scan for you. My receptionist will call you when she gets you an appointment."

"Do you have any idea what these masses are?"

"No. That's why I'm ordering a CT scan," he answered, coldly.

I almost said, *Well Mr. Personality, I sure hope you can figure it out. You're one cold sonofabitch.* For once I kept my big mouth shut.

It took another week before I could get the CT scan. I knew time wasn't on my side, but I couldn't change things to suit myself. I tried to be patient, but I've never been a patient person, and I was being tested beyond my limits.

I had the CT scan done and I was told the results would be sent to Doctor T, and his receptionist would call me when I had an appointment. It took another week before I could see Doctor T for my results.

He came into the exam room, pushing his cart with his laptop on it. The scan images were in front of him along with a written statement in plain English. He coldly said, "You have a dime size umbilical hernia. I'll keep an eye on it. Most likely it won't get any bigger."

"A dime size umbilical hernia would cause all the swelling in my abdomen?" I asked, not believing him for one minute.

"You're not swollen," he said.

I was getting angry, but I kept my composure. "I'm not swollen? My stomach was this size when I was five months pregnant, three times."

He gave a deep sigh with an eye roll. Nobody gives me an eye-roll. I was getting angrier, but I still kept my cool. "What about the four masses in my left side. And the one that just popped up on my right side?"

"Nothing to worry about," he said.

"I worry about it. This isn't right," I said, raising my voice. "You can't tell me there's nothing to worry about. An umbilical hernia wouldn't cause all these masses which are getting bigger."

"I said, I'll keep an eye on the hernia. You need to get a colonoscopy since you've never had one." He closed his laptop and I was dismissed.

Hell has no fury like the kind that was boiling in me. Before he got all the way out of the room, I yelled, "You're a fuckin' idiot!" I don't mean to offend any reader with my strong language, but when I'm boiling with anger the F word will fly out of my mouth. I was beyond furious.

I don't know what the images showed and I wouldn't know if I had seen them since my eyes aren't trained to read them, but the word ascites was plainly written on the report. Evidently, he didn't know the definition of ascites. He didn't mention it.

A week later I went back to my primary doctor and asked him if he would pull up my CT scan on his computer and please explain it. It still amazes me how quickly a doctor can pull up everything on their computers. Within seconds he read the written report to me.

"What is ascites?" I asked.

"It's fluid in the abdominal cavity, usually an indication of cancer cells, but it isn't definite." I could see the look of concern on his face.

When he said cancer, I went numb. It couldn't be cancer. Other people got cancer. Not me. "What should I do now?" I asked, as tears rolled down my face.

"I think you need to see a gynecologist."

"I don't know one in Henderson. Do you know a good one in Evansville that you can refer me to?"

"There is one in Evansville who comes to Henderson once a week. I can refer you to him if you want me to."

"Yes, please do," My mind was not going to accept that I could have cancer. It had to be something else.

Doctor R sent a referral to Doctor F. "They'll call you when they have a date for you."

"Thank you," I managed to say through my tears.

A week later I hadn't heard from Doctor F. I called his office. I was told they didn't have a referral. I explained that Doctor R had sent it in a week ago. The receptionist said it could be my insurance that was holding it up, but she'd call me as soon as she got the referral and give me an appointment.

Another week went by and I didn't get a call. I called Doctor F's office again. They still had no referral. I was getting madder. I gave the receptionist the details of my condition. She said, "I'm so sorry, but I can't make you an appointment with Doctor F without a referral. However, he has a nurse practitioner.

You don't have to be referred to her. Would you like for me to make you an appointment to see her?"

"Dear God, yes!" I said in tears.

It took another week before I could get in to see Nurse K. I was weaker and sicker and some days I couldn't stay out of bed for more than two hours. I managed to drive myself to her office. She carefully listened as I explained my bladder pain and I showed her the masses in my sides. I could tell by the look on her face that she was very concerned. She said she was going to order blood work and an abdominal ultrasound.

I got my blood work done that day, but it was another week before I could be scheduled for the ultrasound. Again, I knew time wasn't on my side but I couldn't change things. I did my best to remain calm and I prayed with all my heart and soul. I was so weak I could barely drive, but I managed to go to the hospital for the ultrasound. My daughters knew I was getting sicker by the day, but I didn't tell them exactly how weak I was. I never want to put worry on my children.

It was the first week of July, and I kept waiting for Nurse K to call me with the results of my blood work, which I knew only took one day. I didn't know how long it would take for her to get the results of my ultrasound. Another week passed. No call. By this time I was so weak it was all I could do to roll out of bed and make it into the bathroom, a few feet away. I wanted to sleep around the clock.

By mid-July, I was in a sound sleep when Nameless came into my bedroom, holding my cell phone and said, "It's a doctor's office."

I snatched the phone. Finally, somebody was going to tell me something.

Nurse K was calling. She didn't mention anything about my ultrasound, or if she did, I didn't hear her. When she gave me my CA-125 count I lost my breath. The normal range is thirty-five or below. Mine was two thousand seventy-five.

I said, "Well, I might as well order my casket. I've got ovarian cancer."

She said, "Now calm down. The blood work isn't a conclusive test. I'll do my best to get you in to see Doctor F as soon as possible."

I dropped the phone. It was conclusive enough for me. I cried for the rest of the day. Two weeks later I still didn't have an appointment to see Doctor F. The ascites was worse and it had gone under my rib cage. I was in unbearable pain.

Chapter Nine

July 30th, 2018, I was so weak I couldn't get out of bed. Nameless helped me get to the bathroom and back to bed. He made sure I had water by my bed, and he did his best to get me to eat. I couldn't eat more than three or four bites. I knew if I forced it down it would come back up.

That night I couldn't sleep and I figured it was because I had slept all day, which I was doing every day. I glanced at the clock on my nightstand. It was midnight. I started praying, asking God to please direct me and tell me what to do. As loudly as if it were beside me, an angel said, "Go to the ER in Owensboro. You're dying."

Through tears, I mumbled, "God, please let me live until morning and I'll get to Owensboro." I don't remember saying amen. I fell into a deep sleep.

The next morning I woke up and the smell of fresh brewing coffee made me want a cup. I managed to get out of bed, and holding on to furniture, I went through the living room and made it into the kitchen. Before I could reach for a cup in the cupboard my head was hanging over the sink and I was heaving.

Nameless ran to me. "What can I do?"

When I could speak, I said, "Call an ambulance. I'm going to the ER in Owensboro."

He said, "I can take you to the ER."

I answered, "Yes, but I'd have to sit in the waiting room for six or eight hours. I'm too weak, I'm in horrible pain and I can't do it. Call an ambulance. I'm having chest pressure and I'm vomiting, which could mean the ascites has gone to my heart and I might be in congestive heart failure."

He held on to me and got me into the living room and I sat down on the sofa. I started heaving again. He ran into the kitchen and brought me a pan to hold in my lap. I was dry heaving and it felt as if my guts were trying to come out of my mouth. He called an ambulance.

When the ambulance arrived, I told them about the pressure in my chest. Then I grabbed the pan in my lap and heaved. When I could talk, I told the MT to take me to Owensboro. He said he didn't have authorization to take me there. I said, "Fine. I'll sit right here on this sofa and die! I'm not about to go to the ER in this town. If I'm not dead by the time I get there I soon will be!"

The MT asked me my age. I told him I was seventy-five. He made a call. Whomever he was talking with told him to take me to Owensboro. The MT and the driver put me on a gurney, still heaving. However, the pressure in my chest had let up.

The ambulance pulled out of the driveway and I said to the MT. "Aren't you going to start an IV?"

"Yes, ma'am, I'm getting it ready."

"You mean you're going to start an IV with this ambulance rolling. The driver is going to hit every pothole in the road. This thing is like riding in a covered wagon."

He patted my hand. "I've done it many times en route. Please stay calm and I'll have it done in a few minutes." He handed me a plastic barf bag. "As soon as I'm in a vein I'll give you a dose of Phrygian. That should stop the heaves."

He was good. He had the IV going, quickly. He injected Phrygian, and within a few minutes the heaves stopped. However, it made me loopy and I was talking, as the old saying goes, a mile a minute. I told him about the doctors I'd seen, the test that had been done and the runaround I'd been through in the past three months. He just nodded his head.

I said, "By using my mouth, I've shot up two doctors, a lab tech, and a radiologist. Let me tell you, they were all ducking for cover. Nobody wants to fool with me when my mouth goes off, it's worse than a cannon."

He laughed and said, "I can only imagine."

My mouth was still in full gear. "A funny thing happened when I went for my CT scan. The tech opened the door to the waiting room and called my name. I got up. But a man in front of me got up and was at the door before me. The tech looked at him, back at the chart, then at me a bit confused. I said,

'I'm the one you want. And if there is a man here with my name we've got a problem.'

"All he had to do was check my wristband, but he continued to look at us. I held up my right wrist. 'This might help. That's why they put them on patients.' He checked my wristband and told me to follow him. I don't think he appreciated my comment. I didn't care. A lab tech did the same thing. She called my name but she didn't check my wristband to see if my name and birth date matched the requisition on her computer. I called her on it. That's why I said my mouth had shut up a lab tech and a radiologist."

The ride to Owensboro seemed to be one hundred miles. So I continued talking. I looked at the MT and said, "I got on my computer and went to WebMD. I typed in my symptoms. They wrote back. 'You are dead. Go toward the light.' Should I get a second opinion?"

"You're too much, girl. But yes, I'd get a second opinion which we are about to do."

The driver pulled the ambulance under the canopy of the ER. The MT and driver opened the back doors. Just as they had me out of the ambulance, Nameless walked up to them. The MT said, "This woman is a hoot."

I mumbled, "Glad I could entertain you. I'll be here all week."

Things were a blur as I was pushed down several long hallways and pushed into a room. The MT picked me up as if I were a baby and placed me on the bed in the ER. He wished me well, patted my hand, and I could see the look of concern on his face. He knew I was a very sick woman.

Within minutes two nurses were by my side. One undressed me and put a hospital gown on me which I could wrap around my body ten times. Then she set up a monitor machine and she put oxygen tubes up my nose. The other one was taking out the IV lock the MT had put in and she was doing her best to find a better vein. Another nurse came in with a computer and the interrogation began. I gave her all the information. When I told her how high my CA-125 count was I saw her raise her eyebrows. I knew she knew what I'd already figured out. I had ovarian cancer.

By the time I had answered all the questions, my two daughters, Cathye and Michelle, and my two oldest granddaughters, Christina and Crystal, rushed into the room, tears rolling. I had to be a strong mother and grandmother. I hid my fear and said, "Listen to me, babies. I'm going to be fine. I'm in a good place and they'll figure out what to do for me."

Before I finished my speech my youngest granddaughter, Julia, had made it to the hospital and she came running to my side. She didn't say anything, she just held my hand. I could feel the strong love flowing from her into me. I've always believed that love is the best medicine. The love I felt from my family was overwhelming.

I hadn't been there long before the ER doctor came in. She had read the answers to all the questions the nurse had typed, and she had gotten the results of my CT scan, my abdominal ultrasound and blood work from Henderson. She ordered another CT scan and more blood work. When she got the results back, she came into my room.

"I've contacted two surgeons and asked if they would drain the ascites. Both said no. I've called a third one but I'm pretty sure the answer is going to be no. Draining ascites is a tricky thing."

She paused for a minute. "If you have no objections I'd like to have you transported by ambulance to the University of Louisville Medical Center."

I said, "Send me anywhere you want to. I need doctors who know what they're dealing with and know how to do their jobs. I already know I have ovarian cancer. I want the best treatment I can get."

She patted my hand. "We don't know for sure it's ovarian cancer. Only a biopsy will give us the answer. I'll get the paper work started to have you transported. There's a lot of red tape to get through, but I'll do my best and as quickly as I can."

By the time my family and I agreed on transporting me to Louisville, a nurse came into the room and told the ER doctor that Doctor W was on the phone. She left the room. A few minutes later she came back. "Doctor W, a great surgeon said he would drain the ascites later today. Do you want him to do it, or do you want to go on to Louisville? And going to Louisville means I have to get the paper work through and get everything approved which may take a day or more."

My children and I agreed to let Doctor W drain the ascites. We didn't want to wait another hour, let alone another day. And my children didn't want me a three-hour drive away if a doctor in Owensboro could do it.

The ER doctor admitted me. It was 4 p.m. by the time I was taken to the 6th floor. Hospital beds are miserable and I was hungry and thirsty. I did my best to keep my spirits up, and laugh and joke with my children and grandchildren. We all told stories about all the silly things I'd done with them when they were growing up. And they confessed their sins that had gotten past me. By 8 p.m., Doctor W was still in surgery. I lost my laughing spirit. I said, "Screw this shit. I'm going to eat."

My youngest daughter, Michelle, said, "Screw it is right. If he's still in surgery at eight o'clock at night, he's too tired for me to agree to let him do surgery on you."

My oldest daughter, Cathye, said, "She's right." She picked up the cafeteria menu and read it to me. "What do you want me to order?"

"Just order me a bowl of tomato soup. I'm nauseous, but I think I can keep it down."

She laughed and said, "Why not order a club sandwich to go with it. I know you won't eat it, but I'm the pig in the family and I'll eat for you."

Finally, I was able to laugh again. I said, "Order two club sandwiches and two bowls of soup. I know you love to eat. But if you don't mind, please share with Michelle."

Michelle declined. She's like me. When I'm upset I can't eat. She was worried along with being angry with Doctor W.

A nurse came into my room at 9 p.m., and said, "Doctor W is about ready for you."

I said, "Screw him! I was tired of starving and I ate."

As soon as the nurse left the room, Doctor W came in. "I was getting an OR room ready for you, but the nurse told me you ate. I don't appreciate patients who go against my orders."

I said, "For two days I've starved while I waited for you. I understand you had emergencies, but there's only so long I can hold on. Do you mind to explain the procedure?"

He said, "I'm going to make a small incision on the right bottom side of your abdomen and drain enough ascites to send for a biopsy. And I'll do a biopsy on your ovary, which I'll do laparoscopic and pull it through your belly-button."

"Why are you going to do it on the right side? My left side is where the ascites is?"

"Look. Don't tell me how to do my job. You asked me to explain what I was going to do, and I did. That's how it's going to be. I don't argue with patients!"

"I wasn't arguing. I was simply asking questions. I thought it was my right."

"I answered your questions. I'll do your surgery tomorrow, but you better not go against me again!" With that, he left the room. That was the beginning of my bad relationship with Doctor W.

Michelle had been posting on Facebook, updating my friends on my condition. The outpouring of love and prayers for me was overwhelming. At this point things weren't looking good, but I wasn't going to have a pity party. I was going to laugh, joke, and be my silly self.

came for me. By 2:30 I was getting frustrated. Two days in a row I had been starved and I was thirsty. I tried to make light of the situation and I had quite a strong stoma and not show my children how scared I was. "I know neither of you will slip me an ice cube, but would you mind spitting in to my mouth?"

They laughed but refused my request. We were still watching the clock. When 3:00 rolled around, my daughters went out of my room, and to say they were furious would be an understatement. They went to the nurse's station and asked why nobody had taken me. The nurse told them that Doctor W was doing an emergency surgery and would get to me as soon as he could.

By six o'clock that night I was still waiting, saying aloud, "I may die but I'm going to eat." As I was eating a bag of chips and washing them down with a full glass of water, a nurse came into my room and said that Doctor W would get to me as soon as possible. "Sorry but I'm eating," I said and I tucked a chip into my mouth.

The nurse gave me a blank stare and said, "He's not happy with you. It's good to stay on his good side."

"I'm not very happy with him, so that makes us even. As for his good side, I'm not in to play on my good side."

Michelle said, "And he isn't going to operate on my mother after being in surgery all day. He's tired.

Chapter Ten

My two oldest granddaughters had to go home to take care of their children, and my youngest grand-daughter had to go to work. My daughters Cathye and Michelle refused to leave me. They were going to sleep on the two benches in my room. I firmly said, "You two go home. You're worn out and I'm in good hands. Now don't argue with me. Mama has spoken!"

Before they left, a nurse came into my room and said that Doctor W would take me to the OR at 2:30 p.m., the next day. We were relieved. They went home and assured me they would be back before I was taken into surgery.

A nurse had explained to us that this was a dangerous procedure. A surgeon has to be precise in making an incision. One fraction off the mark and my intestines would be punctured. This was a bit scary, but I put myself in God's hands and asked Him to guide the surgeon's hands. However, I was anxious to get it done, hoping I'd get relief from the pain, but mostly to find out what a biopsy would tell me.

The next morning my daughters were there. We laughed, talked, and kept watching the hands click by on the wall clock. I was supposed to be taken to OR prep at 1:30 p.m.. Time rolled around and nobody came for me. By 2:30 I was getting frustrated. Two days in a row I had been starved and I was thirsty. I tried to make light of the situation. I still had to be a strong mama and not show my children how scared I was. "I know neither of you will slip me an ice cube, but would you mind spitting in my mouth?"

They laughed, but refused my request. We were still watching the clock. When 3:30 rolled around, my daughters went out of my room, and to say they were furious would be an understatement. They went to the nurse's station and asked why nobody had come for me. The nurse told them that Doctor W was doing an emergency surgery and he'd get to me as soon as he could.

By eight o'clock that night I was still waiting. Again, I said, "Screw this shit. I'm going to eat." As I was eating a bag of chips and washing them down with a tall glass of water, a nurse came into my room and said that Doctor W would get to me as soon as possible. "Screw him. I'm eating," I said as I stuffed a chip into my mouth.

The nurse gave me a hard stare and said, "He's not happy with you. It's best to stay on his good side."

"I'm not very happy with him so that makes us even. As for his good side, he needs to stay on my good side."

Michelle said, "And he isn't going to operate on my mother after being in surgery all day. He's tired.

Mama is tired and he can either do it the first thing in the morning or we'll find another surgeon. This is bullshit!"

Nurse said, "He's the only surgeon in Owensboro who's been trained to do this procedure. So unless you want to go to another hospital, you need to stay with him."

I said, "I'll stay with him. At this point I don't have any choice."

Nurse said, "I'll be back in a few minutes and tell you what Doctor W says."

We waited an hour and nobody told us a thing. Michelle was about to explode. Cathye said, "Let me handle this, Sis." She went to the nurse's station. She came back to my room and said I was scheduled for 7:30 a.m. And I would be taken for OR prep by 6:30. I had my doubts after being put off for two days, but I prayed he wouldn't let me down.

The next morning my daughters were at the hospital a few minutes before I was taken for OR prep. They kissed me, told me they loved me and they would be praying for me during surgery.

I'm not the crying type, but at that moment tears were rolling. I was scared. I managed to say through tears, "I love you with all my heart. You just pray and Mama will be fine."

My tears continued to roll. I couldn't control them. However, when I got to the OR prep room, the nurses were so kind and sweet they put some of my fears to rest.

Doctor W came into the prep room and said, "An OR room is being cleaned for you. It won't be long."

I said, "Doctor W, if you don't mind would you please have a nurse put a catheter in me. After I go under anesthesia my bladder is numb for twelve hours—"

He cut me off in mid-sentence. "No! There's no reason for a catheter. I'm not going to take a chance on an infection."

"I've never gotten an infection from being catheterized. I—"

He didn't let me finish my sentence. He held up his hand and raised his voice. "I said there will be no catheter. I won't argue with you!" He quickly walked out of the room.

I looked at the nurses and said, "Doctor W doesn't like me and to be honest I don't like him. I hope I piss all over him during surgery."

They laughed. "You're a hoot," one nurse said. "He's hard to get along with at times, but he's a good surgeon and you're in good hands."

While I was in recovery, Doctor W came into the waiting room and spoke with my daughters. This is a direct quote from him. "She did fine. She'll be in her room in an hour. Your mother is very confrontational, and I don't put up with that!"

If either daughter replied to him, I wasn't told. They know what to tell me and what not to. He also told them he drained a liter of ascites and he did a biopsy of my left ovary. He explained it would be two weeks before the results came back, and his office would call me for a post-op appointment and I'd get the results of the biopsies then.

I was taken back to my hospital room by ten o'clock. My daughters were on either side of my bed, each holding my hands. I was fully awake and I have no words to describe how happy I was to see their sweet faces. They took turns feeding me ice chips. I didn't want food. They did their best to coax me to take a few sips of tomato soup, but I couldn't. Nausea was telling me it wouldn't stay down. I was getting an anti-nausea medication through my IV, but it wasn't doing much good.

During the two days I was waiting for surgery an oncologist, Doctor M came in to see me twice. He didn't mention any course of treatment. He merely made chit-chat. He was from India, spoke broken English and it was hard for me to understand him. However, he was very kind and I liked him. He told me he wanted me to see a gynecologist after I was released from the hospital. I told him that I didn't know a gynecologist in Owensboro. He told me he knew a good one and he'd be happy to refer me to her.

"I give her call. When she get results of biopsies, she call you for consultation."

I was glad to hear I would be seeing a woman.

When he left the room I said, "When he gets the results of my biopsies, he thinks he's going to pump me full of chemo. I'm not taking that shit. It'll do me more harm than good. I've known too many people who took it and all it did was make them sick as a dog and they died anyway."

My daughters didn't say anything. I think at this point they didn't know what to think or who to listen to.

At 2 p.m. a nurse came into my room and told my daughters I had been dismissed. I was shocked and so were they. I thought it was too soon for me to be released, but I was glad to be getting out of the hospital after three days and two nights. I couldn't wait to get home to my comfortable bed.

Michelle and Cathye took me home. They got my prescriptions filled and stayed with me until I went to sleep. The next day they came back. Michelle said, "We're going to pack everything you need and you're going home with me."

I couldn't hold back my tears. I knew Nameless would do his best, but I also knew he didn't know how to take care of me. At this point I was as helpless as a newborn.

August 6th, 2018, I went to live with Michelle. I was happy. I'd get to see Olivia every day. I knew that Tiny Terror was the best medicine I could have.

Olivia was at school when I got there. I was excited about her coming home so I could tell her I was going to be living with her. When she came in from school, Michelle told her that I was in Julia's room. Julia had moved out and was living with a roommate. She was nineteen and she wanted to be on her own.

My heart raced as I heard Olivia's footsteps hurrying into my room. She ran into the room, yelling, "Nana!" But one look at me and she backed away. She didn't want anything to do with a sick old lady in bed. Her fun Nana was gone. I asked her if she wanted to come hold my hand and talk to me. She said, "Not really." Out the door she went.

Tears rolled as I listened to her footsteps leaving me. I understood, but it broke my heart.

Chapter Eleven

I was getting weaker by the day and I was as helpless as a newborn. I lost all control of my bladder and bowels. Michelle bathed me, spoon fed me, changed my Depends full of poop and pee. She did her best to support my weight as she walked me. She knew I had to take a few steps a day and she knew if I stayed in bed all the time the chances were great that I'd develop pneumonia.

With her help I managed to walk the short hallway, twice a day. She took care of me and had a five-year-old to take care of, but she never complained. I could see the tiredness in her eyes and my heart hurt. I prayed that God would continue to give her strength. I knew we still had a long way to go.

I asked her every day to let my Facebook friends know how I was doing. She posted this: "This is Michelle. Mom is not able to get on the computer, but I'll do my best to read to her everything that has been posted on her timeline as well as private messages. They bring a big smile to her face. I don't have time to answer all messages, but know that all comments and messages are being read to my mom and she appreciates them. She also asked me to check her book sales page. Every time she makes a sale, she smiles and I see light come back to her eyes. Thank you for buying her books. With each sale she says, 'I'm two dollars richer.' It's not about the money to her. She's just happy that people are reading her books."

Cathye did her best to come out and take care of me and give Michelle a break, but she wasn't able to come as often as she wanted. When she did come, she took care of me as if I were her child. I couldn't believe I had become the child and my daughters had become the mother. It was a hard pill for me to swallow. I never thought it would ever come to this point, yet here we were and our roles had been reversed. I was grateful, but also sad. I still wanted to be the mother and take care of my babies.

My son would have been by my side all the way. He would have fed me, made sure I had plenty of fluids in me, and he would have changed my poopy Depends with no hesitation. However, he was incarcerated. I was able to talk to him on the phone now and then. He knew I was sick but he didn't know what was wrong. I didn't want him to know at this point. He was under enough pressure and I didn't want him worrying about me. My mother's heart cried for him daily.

I hadn't been to visit him since April, and I knew he had to be told. At this time all he knew was I had a severe upper respiratory infection and a urinary tract infection. My oldest daughter, Cathey and her youngest daughter, Crystal went to visit him. As gently as possible they broke the news to him. Cathye said he hung his head, but he didn't dare cry. When you're an inmate you don't show tears. It's taken as weakness and the inmates will pounce on you. Cathye and Crystal told me that he took the news well, he sent his love and he wanted me to know he'd be praying for me. My mother's heart cried for him.

We had waited a week, anxious to get an appointment with Doctor W. Michelle called his office and got me an appointment the following week. By the end of the first week after surgery, I had gained a little strength, thanks to Michelle and Cathye. They kept enough food and fluids in me to keep me from dehydrating. They still walked me, and Michelle made sure I sat in the recliner. Lying flat on my back night and day was getting to me mentally and physically, but it was the only way the unbearable pain under my rib cage would let up. I tried lying on my sides, but I couldn't. Pains shot through my whole body.

My sister, Linda, also came to help Michelle, and she brought cooked meals. She makes the best cornbread that I've ever eaten. I managed to eat a couple bites but nausea still plagued me. Michelle was thankful for the wonderful meals her aunt Linda brought. She was too tired to do much cooking.

There was a crucifix hanging on my bedroom wall between the outside door and closet door. Michelle had draped a rosary over the crucifix and the cross on the end of it hung a few inches from the crucifix. I touched the small cross every day and prayed.

I was sitting in the recliner one night and Michelle was sitting in a chair a few feet away. I saw her eyes widen. I thought I was turning white or something. Before I could ask what was wrong she said, "Mom, look over your right shoulder."

I turned and my breath caught in my throat. The rosary was swaying in rhythm. There was no air circulating in the room. No fan. No open windows. The rosary wasn't swaying from side to side, it was swaying in and out. The cross on the end of it was casting a shadow on the wall. The shadow didn't move. Only the cross at the end of the rosary. I smiled and a warm glow spread through my body. I said, "That's God, Jesus, angels, and holy spirits telling me that love and prayers that are being sent up from family and friends are being heard and answered."

"I think you're right," she answered, and I saw her eyes leak.

Me being me, added, "Or it's the angels coming to get me. If I'm not here in the morning you know where I am."

"Mom, God and the devil are still arguing over which one has to take you. So I think you'll be here for a while."

We both laughed, but we took it as a sign that I would be fine and I had nothing to worry about.

Three days passed and it was time for my visit with Doctor W. I also had an appointment to see two more doctors the same day, each within an hour of each visit. One was for a consultation with a gynecologist, Doctor A, and one with my oncologist, Doctor M.

I was weak and tired but I was full of hope and glad I'd get all appointments taken care of on the same day. I prayed that I'd have the strength to hold out. The ride to Owensboro was rough, but I hung on, gritting my teeth from the pain under my rib cage. We arrived at Doctor W's office. Cathye and Michelle held onto both my arms. Using all the strength I had and using them for support, I made it into the waiting room.

I was nervous but since I'd only had symptoms for three months, I figured my cancer would be stage one or at worst stage two. My next appointment was with my gynecologist. I hoped she would schedule me for surgery soon and once she took out my rotten ovary, I'd be fine.

A nurse called my name. Both daughters held onto my arms and escorted me into the exam room. The nurse told me to sit on the table and Doctor W would be with me shortly. I sat down and thought, *it better be shortly. I'm not about to sit here until eight o'clock.* By the time the thought ran through my mind, Doctor W came into the room. He sat down in a chair close to the exam table next to me. My heart was racing.

"Your biopsies came back. You have stage three ovarian cancer and the ascites is full of cancer cells, which are attacking your liver and colon. The only hope you have is to take chemo."

My mind was screaming, *God no. It can't be.* I broke down and cried harder than I can remember. Both daughters gathered me in their arms as I sobbed so hard my body was shaking. Both of them told me that I was the strongest woman they had ever known and I'd fight the cancer and I'd win.

When I could talk, I looked at Doctor W. "Do you think I have a fighting chance?"

He held up his left hand as if it were a stop sign and coldly said, "I don't know. I'm not God."

My anger flared but he had also hurt my feelings and I couldn't say a word. I knew that I was nothing more to him than a number, another one that he had to deliver bad news to. All in a day's work.

He stood up and said, "Make an appointment to get a colonoscopy done before you leave."

I asked, "Who is going to do it?" I thought only gastroenterologists did colonoscopies.

"I will," he flatly stated and left the room.

My daughters took my arms and we left the exam room. When we reached the nurses' station, Michelle said, "Mom, hang on to Cathye and I'll make your appointment."

"The hell you will. That cold-hearted bastard will never touch me again. Just get me to the car and over to Doctor A's office."

Neither daughter said anything. They aided me along to the car. They knew Mama had spoken and that's how it would be. When we were on our way, I said, "I need surgery to get my rotten ovary out. I'll worry about a colonoscopy later, but he sure won't be doing it."

They agreed.

They aided me into Doctors A's office. The devastating news I had just received was more painful than the pain under my rib cage. We didn't have to wait long and a nurse called me back to Doctor A's office.

Doctor A pulled up the results of my biopsies and notes from Doctor W, on her computer. She looked at me and said, "I know you came in for a consultation for surgery. You're in no condition for surgery, you wouldn't survive it. Your *only* hope is to start chemo." She wished me well and I could see the look of concern in her eyes. She was kind, caring, and I liked her.

We left Doctor A's office and we were on our way see Doctor M. My body was trembling, my mind was spinning, but with the aid of my daughters, I made it.

I was called back to his office by the time I got settled in a chair. My daughters held on to me and I did what I call a Tim Conway shuffle. I was so tired I couldn't put one foot in front of the other. Doctor M was in his office waiting for me when we came through the door. He greeted us with a handshake and told me to have a seat in the chair across from his desk. My daughters pulled up chairs and were sitting next to me.

Doctor M explained, "I start you on strong chemo, but I only give you half dose at time because you too small to take full dose. You take treatment once a week for two weeks, then you get a week break. Then you do two more and get a week break. You have to take eight infusions."

My daughters looked at me and together they said, "Mom, are you going to take the chemo?"

I held their hands and said, "One more time, I'll eat my words. If I want to live, and I do, then I'll take chemo."

Doctor M said, "That good. I schedule you for PET scan this Friday. You get scan done, then go to infusion room and take first round of chemo. You do a total of eight rounds. The chemo will kill cancer cells in abdominal fluid and shrink the tumors on your ovaries. I hope by at least mid-November, you be strong enough to undergo surgery to remove ovaries and drain the fluid."

"Doctor M, don't I need a port?"

"No. I don't like ports. I don't take chance on blood clots or infection. I use veins."

"I have poor veins," I said.

"The nurses are very good. They find veins. No worry."

I left the office numb to the bone. A part of me was still in denial. I didn't have cancer. Another part knew I had to accept my fate and do whatever it took to save me.

Note from my journal: Cancer is like a thief in the night. It comes and strikes. It takes you down fast and hard. Cancer will not defeat me. I'll fight with all I have. I'll beat this monster.

Chapter Twelve

Note from my journal: August 9, 2018. I am no longer a skinny mini. My stomach is so swollen it looks like a tick that's been sucking on a dog for six months. I have to wear my sister's oversize PJ's. When I go to the doctor I put my terrycloth robe on, slip on socks and put my house slippers on. The air conditioning in doctors' offices is so cold I freeze, so my heavy robe feels good. As soon as I leave the building I pull off my robe and head across the parking lot in my PJ's. I got strange looks. I didn't care. Maybe I gave people their laugh for the day.

Facebook post: August 10, 2018. My precious friends I've read all your comments and private messages. My heart overflows with love and peace by your responses. I don't have the strength to comment on them, but I do read them a few at a time. Most of them make me cry, because I can feel your love and I know your hearts are full of prayers for me. I'm nobody special, but you love me enough to hold me up in prayer and well wishes. Thank you so much, and know my heart and prayers are with you. I'm very tired and I'll probably go to bed soon, but I'll try to read what comes in tomorrow. I'm fighting with all my soul. I have a long battle ahead of me. I *will* win! God bless you all.

Note from my journal: August 12th, 2018. Since I go everywhere in my PJ's and robe, Olivia thinks she should be allowed to do the same thing. A little talk from her mother and she quickly found out that she wouldn't. She stomped her foot and said, "Well, shoot a monkey! I wanted to be like Nana."

Note from my journal: August 15th 2018, I've been living with Michelle and Olivia for two weeks. Olivia is warming up to me. I'm getting out of bed, walking and sitting in the recliner. I figure she takes this as a sign that I'm more than just a sick old lady who stays in bed all day. When Michelle walks me down the hallway, Olivia leads the way. She counts each step and she thinks it's a game. She's also coming into my room and talking to me. Her sweet face and voice make my heart happy and I know if I'm going to the win the cancer battle, she's my best medicine. When it's bedtime, she comes into my bedroom with Michelle. She pulls the blankets up under my chin, then she tucks the blankets under both my sides. She says she's making a burrito. I said, "Nana likes it when you make her into a burrito." She gives me a kiss and she insisted that she be the one to turn out the lamp on the bedside table. I fall asleep with her sweet face flashing through my mind. I can still hear her sweet voice as I say my prayers.

August 17th, 2018, I went for my first PET scan. They injected me with radioactive iodine and I had to lay back in a recliner for an hour. Then I was taken to a room and placed into what I called a metal tunnel. I had to hold both arms over my head and not move for thirty minutes as the tunnel went in and out making crazy sounds. My arms ached and trembled, but I managed to stay put and not move for the duration. I called it the torture tunnel.

After I was *nuked*, I went to the chemo infusion center. The receptionist put a wristband on me. I had no idea what to expect and I was a bit nervous. I never let on to Michelle that I had any fear. I laughed, joked, and went into the room that I called the interrogation room. One nurse asked questions and typed my answers. The other nurse started an IV and drew blood. My veins had been blown so many times when I was in the hospital she had a hard time finding one that would hold. After two tries, she found a good one. I had an IV pole with a monitor attached. Tubes and wires were in every direction.

A nurse pushed my pole, and Michelle held onto my arm as we went to a private room with a private restroom. The room was decorated with beautiful pictures hanging on the walls. It had two large windows and I could see the beauty of many trees and the pretty sky. I thought I was in a hotel. The bed looked like a regular hospital bed with all the buttons you can push to adjust your head and legs. I lay down and I couldn't believe how comfortable it was. I brought my pillow with me because I figured any pillow the center had wouldn't be comfortable. I used the pillow that was on the bed to put under my knees. I was comfortable and ready to start my treatment.

A nurse came into the room and hung a bag on the IV pole. She said it was an anti-nausea medication. When the bag emptied, a beeper on the monitor went off. A few minutes later the nurse came back, took down the empty bag and hung another one. She said it was another anti-nausea med with Decadron. When that bag emptied and the beeper went off, two nurses came in. They were gowned and masked. I said, "You don't have to hide your faces. I know who you are."

They laughed and one nurse said, "We have to put on gowns and masks when we bring the chemo."

At this point I was a bit more nervous. Chemo was powerful stuff if they had to gown and mask. I wondered how it was going to affect me as it went through my veins and made its course through my body. And I wondered why it took two nurses. I soon found out. They make no mistakes.

Both asked me my name and birth date. I answered. They looked at my wristband, then scanned it. Both checked the information on my wristband

and looked at the computer screen, making sure I was the right person and they were giving me the right chemo. I was more at ease. It took one hour for the bag to empty.

With all the fluids running through me I had to pee every twenty minutes. I still didn't have complete control of my bladder, but with Michelle's help I made it to the restroom before I filled my Depends. Michelle had to unplug my machine, push it with one hand and hold my arm with her other hand.

By the time we made it to the restroom and back, all the wires and tubes were twisted around the pole. The wheels on the pole wanted to go one way and Michelle and I wanted to go the other way. Michelle twisted the pole, untangled everything that had wrapped around it, and finally got me back in bed. "Mom, I sure hope you slow down with your peeing. I'm not sure how many times I can untangle this stuff before I wrap it around your leg."

"I know it's hard to do, honey, but I can't hold my pee and we didn't bring an extra Depends. You're doing great. Just don't get the wires or tubes wrapped around my neck and we'll be fine."

The beeper went off. The hour had gone by quickly as Michelle and I laughed and joked and I cut up with the nurses. It was time for the second bag of chemo. Again, two nurses came into the room gowned and masked, and we went through the same verifications.

As the second bag of chemo was running through me, I prayed with every drop I saw come from the bag and run into the tube. "Dear God, please let this stuff eat the cancer." Michelle prayed with me.

The second bag emptied and I was glad to get out of there. Michelle didn't have a comfortable chair and I knew she was happier to go than I was. However, she never complained. While we were there they brought us ham and cheese sandwiches and potato chips. Michelle ate all of hers. I nibbled. When we were handed my discharge papers, a nurse asked if we'd like to have something to drink to take with us. They had tea, sodas, lemonade, and water. When she said sodas, my taste buds wanted a Dr. Pepper. It had been years since I'd had one. I had stopped drinking sodas because of the amount of sugar they contained. I called soda, death in a can.

The nurse brought me a glass of ice and I poured the Dr. Pepper in it. I never could drink anything out of a can. I took a sip and it was heavenly. I didn't figure one soda a week would hurt me.

We got on the elevator and pushed the button for the first floor. "One down and seven to go, Mom."

"I just hope I don't have a bad reaction to the chemo. I know I've got my Phenergan and Compazine, but I'm not sure—"

"Mom, we'll worry about that when the time comes. They gave you anti-nausea meds in your IV. Stop getting uptight."

"I'm sorry. I just overthink things. I'll be fine." I prayed that I was right. However, I felt stronger coming out than when I went in. Then I remember I had been given Decadron. I was jacked up on steroids.

Olivia was waiting at the door when we came in. She hugged me and said, "Daddy said Mommy took you to the doctor to get medicine. Are you gonna get well?"

I hugged her tightly. "Yes, honey. But it'll take a long time before I'm all the way well. I have to go to the doctor and take more medicine every week. I feel better though."

"Good. Do you want to play cards with me? I want to play War."

"I'll do my best, honey." We went into her play room and we sat at the card table. I was amazed that I could hold out long enough to play two games of War. She beat me both times and she told me I was a losser. A word she had made up when a person lost a game with her. "Yep, Nana is a losser. I don't mind."

The ascites under my rib cage had me in unbearable pain, but I gritted my teeth and played cards with my precious baby. By the end of the second game the pain was so bad I was in tears. The only way I could get relief was to lay flat on my back. Olivia was ready for game three, but I told her that Nana's side was hurting and I needed to rest in my room.

"Are you gonna go to bed, Nana?"

"Yes, honey. But when my side stops hurting I'll play another game with you."

She walked me to my bedroom. She pulled the blankets up under my chin. "You rest, Nana. I'm gonna sit in the recliner and watch Spongebob. But don't close your eyes."

"I'll keep my eyes open and watch Spongebob with you."

She climbed into the recliner and turned on the TV. I noticed she kept glancing over at me from time to time. Since my eyes were open, she continued to watch her program. I didn't realize I had closed my eyes until I heard her jump out of the recliner, run out of the room and close the door. I had no idea what upset her if I closed my eyes, but she wouldn't stay in the room with me at any time if my eyes were closed.

Michelle came into my room an hour later with a bowl of homemade potato soup. She makes the best that I've ever eaten. I sat in the recliner and I managed to eat half of it. My stomach still didn't want much food at one time.

As the week passed on by I was eating more and Michelle was forcing me to drink Ginger Ale. I never did like Ginger Ale, but I knew I needed it. I had drunk all the water I could stand. The ale was a good substitute.

The next Friday it was time for my second round of chemo. I had done well with nausea. I wasn't as nervous. We arrived on time and went through the same procedure as the first time. While the nurse was trying to find a vein in my right arm, Doctor M came into the room. "You look good. Your color is good. I check on you later. Bye."

The nurse found a vein and I was hooked up to an IV pole with a monitor and taken to a room. Before the first bag of anti-nausea meds was finished my arm was hurting. I told the nurse. She looked at my IV site and said, "It's okay. These things are uncomfortable." She hung the second bag and left the room.

As the minutes passed, my arm was hurting worse. I knew something was wrong. I pushed the call button. The nurse came in and I told her my arm was hurting worse and I thought the vein had blown. She checked it and said, "It's fine." And left the room.

I thought I was being foolish so I gritted my teeth. Before the second bag was empty, I raised my right arm. "Michelle, my arm is swelling and I've got purple spots around the swelling. Please get the nurse."

The nurse came back in and looked at my arm. "It looks fine to me."

Michelle walked up to my bedside and picked up my right arm. "Do you mean to tell me that you can't see the swelling and the purple spots? You get the IV out of her arm, now!"

The nurse left the room and soon another nurse came in. She looked at my arm. "The vein is blown. I'll do my best to find a vein in your left arm. The swelling is because your meds weren't going into your vein. They were running under your skin. Your body will absorb them and they'll go into your system. I'll get a warm towel and wrap your arm as soon as I get another IV going."

The nurse found a vein in my left arm. I prayed it wouldn't blow before the chemo bags were empty. The vein held. When it was over, Michelle and I got our Dr. Pepper to go and we were on our way. "Two down and six more to go," I said. "But I don't feel as good this time as I did the first time."

"Hang in there, Mom. Chemo doesn't work that fast. They said the more treatments you take the better you'll feel. We'll see what tomorrow brings."

"I'm hanging on the best I can, honey. I'm going to fight like hell to win this battle."

Chapter Thirteen

The next day I didn't feel well, but I pushed with all I had to walk the hallway three times a day. Again, I wanted to sleep around the clock. Michelle forced food, water, and Ginger Ale down me. I didn't want anything and my taste buds felt as if they had been scraped with sandpaper. I bore up and got down as much food and liquid as I could.

The cancer center had given me a case of Boost Plus and I was supposed to drink a carton three times a day. I hated the taste but I forced it down. I didn't feel like playing with Olivia and again, she was shying away from me. My heart broke. I prayed night and day for God to give me strength and to let the chemo cure me.

The next morning, Michelle brought my Boost to me. "Mom, you need to sit in the recliner and drink it. I know you don't like it, but it's a necessary evil."

"I think I want to sit at the kitchen table. I enjoy looking out the window and seeing the lake. You know how much I love that lake."

I went into the kitchen, pulled out a chair, sat down and sipped the Boost. I managed to get it all down. Just as I was about to say something about the green algae on the lake my stomach churned. I hurried to the kitchen sink and made it just in time to throw up. I heaved until I thought I'd pass out.

Michelle wiped my face and neck with a cold cloth until I could stand upright.

"I bet I never drink that shit again. It's bad enough going down and it's worse coming back up."

"Come on and let me get you back to bed. I'll bring you a bottle of Ginger Ale and give you a Phenergan."

For the rest of the day I kept throwing up. Michelle alternated Phenergan and Compazine every four hours. The pills slowed the vomiting, but they didn't stop it. By 10 p.m., I was so weak I couldn't lift my head off my pillow. When Michelle heard me gag, she put her arm under my shoulders, lifted my head and held a pan for me to vomit in. By this time nothing was coming up except the Ginger Ale. Then I had dry heaves. To me a dry heave is worse than something coming up. It's painful.

When the heaving stopped, she laid me down. "Mom, if you throw up again I'm taking you to the ER."

"I think I'm done. I'm going to sleep. You need to go to bed. You're worn out."

She sat down in the recliner and pushed herself back as far as it would go. "I'm staying right here. All night. I'm not going to take a chance on you vomiting in your sleep and aspirating. You can't lie on your sides and lying flat on your back is a sure way to die."

I knew not to argue. She wasn't about to leave me. Thankfully, I slept through the night and didn't vomit. I woke up when I heard Olivia arguing with Michelle about what she was going to wear to school. My nausea seemed to be gone. "Thank you God for answering my prayers. You got me through the night. Please get me through this day."

After Olivia was off to school, Michelle came into my room. "How do you feel?"

"I'm feeling better. I think I want to sit up in the office chair and look out the window. I love to look at the trees, the birds, and that fat squirrel that runs up and down the power line. He's the size of a cat. He amuses me."

"Marcus likes to watch him too. I'll get you in the chair, then I'll get you a Boost. You know you have to drink it."

"Don't even say that word to me. I won't be drinking any more. Do you have any Carnation Instant Breakfast?"

"Yes, I've got some. I'll fix it for you."

The fat squirrel seemed to know I was watching him and he'd stop and look at me as if he were saying, "Good morning."

Michelle brought me my breakfast and it tasted as good as my taste buds would allow. The pain under my rib cage was bad, but I was determined to sit in the chair and enjoy the beauty outside. Michelle sat down in the recliner and we both laughed at the fat squirrel. Suddenly, my bowels released. "Oh, my God. I just shit all over myself!" I said.

"Well, I'll get you in the shower, clean you up and put a clean Depends on you."

I couldn't hold back my tears. "I'm so sorry, honey. Yesterday, you had to hold my head over a pan all day while I puked my guts up, now you've got to clean me up because I'm shitting my brains out."

"Mom, please don't cry. I don't mind. It's not like it's the first time I've cleaned up a shitty diaper. I did have two babies, ya know. Now, don't say anymore. I know it's humiliating, but I'm your daughter. You changed my shitty diapers for a few years."

For the rest of the day I had diarrhea. I didn't feel it coming and I had no control of my bowels. I was so humiliated I couldn't hold back my tears. At this point I began to think it would be best for me and my kids if I just died. Michelle was getting as many Lomotil down me as she dared without overdosing me. Lomotil slowed the diarrhea but it didn't stop it for two days.

I was so weak I couldn't get out of bed. I couldn't walk three steps without my knees buckling. Michelle managed to hold my head up and get sips of Ginger Ale down me, and she got Carnation Instant Breakfast down me once a day. She did her best to keep me hydrated.

The third night, Michelle held my head up and I managed to swallow a Lomotil. I prayed it would stop my diarrhea. I knew I couldn't last much longer. She kissed me, turned off the lamp and told me to yell if I needed her. Her bedroom was only a few feet from mine. "I love you, Mom," she said as she shut my door.

"I love you, honey. With all my heart." I closed my eyes. I knew I was dying. I don't know how to explain how I knew, I just knew. I lay flat on my back and I tried to pray. Before I could say, "Dear God," I felt life draining from my body. The only way I know how to describe this feeling is to imagine standing in water up to your thighs at high tide, then slowly watch the water ebb until you're standing on wet sand and you're still watching the water ebb further. I couldn't move any part of my body. I just lay and continued to feel life draining from me. I had no fear.

Suddenly, I saw angels. They were standing in a semicircle, like people stand in the choir at church. They were beautiful. They were singing, but in a language I didn't understand. After they sang, they spread their wings and lifted them up toward me as if they were trying to encircle me. I tried to reach out to them, but I couldn't move any part of my body.

The angels continued to hold their wings up high and out toward me for a few seconds. I didn't know if they were welcoming me Home, or if it was their way of saying, "We are here to protect you and keep you safe and sound."

I managed to blink. They were gone. When they disappeared, I felt life coming back into my body. It was a warm glow that started at my toes and slowly rose up through my entire body. When the glow reached my head I wondered if I was wearing a halo.

At that moment I realized I could move my arms, my legs, and I could open my eyes. I looked around the room. The moonlight was shining through the window and I was aware that I was alive. I wasn't under the influence of any strong pain meds. I wasn't dehydrated, which can cause illusions. I wasn't dreaming. It was real. I'd read about near death stories and they were basically the same. You slide down a dark tunnel. You see a bright light. You see your loved ones and other heavenly things. Some say they hear a voice telling them it's not their time. All I saw and heard was a choir of angels.

I didn't mention my near death, or my out-of-body experience to anybody. I was still trying to figure out what the angels were trying to tell me.

After Olivia was off to school, Michelle can into my room to check on me. "How do you feel?"

"I'm not sure, but I'm going to get out of bed and try to walk a few steps. I can't just lie here. I've got to move and try to build my strength. The longer I lay, the weaker I'm going to get."

"You've got a week break before you have to go for another treatment. Are you going to take one?"

"I'll tell you this, if I don't get a port put in so this won't happen again, then you can bet your ass I won't take anymore. I have the right to refuse any treatment that I don't want."

"I'm with you on this. He should have had a surgeon put a port in before you started chemo. Everybody I've ever known who has or is taking chemo has a port. So, if Doctor M wants to give you a hard time, then we'll find a doctor who will agree to one. For two days I held you and wondered if every breath you took might be your last one."

"Oh, honey. I had no idea you were that scared. I'm so sorry." I held back my tears and said, "But here I am. The devil can't have me yet."

She smiled, but she didn't respond. I couldn't begin to imagine what a horrible feeling it would be for a child to hold their mother, wondering which breath would be her last one. I didn't tell her about the angels holding their wings out to me. I thought I'd tell her later when I thought the time was right. And I wasn't sure if I would ever tell her. I had to give it a lot of thought.

Friday, we went back to the cancer center. I refused the chemo infusion. I told the nurses what I'd been through and I wasn't going to take another treatment until I got a port. The nurse said, "You're the boss. If you want a port, then you'll get one. Doctor M will be in to see you soon."

"Back me up, Michelle. You know he's not going to like it."

"I've got your back. He can like it or lump it. Like the nurse said, you're the boss."

Doctor M came in. "What you problem?"

"My veins are no good. All of them have been blown. I want a port put in."

"It not good to miss treatment. You not going to take chemo today?"

"No, I'm not."

"Okay. I'll call Doctor W and get an appointment for a port."

"Oh, no! Doctor W will never touch me again. I don't know another surgeon in Owensboro, but—"

The nurse interrupted. "Doctor N is a great surgeon. He's put in almost all the ports in our patients."

Doctor M asked, "Why you don't like Doctor W? He a good surgeon"

Before I could say he's an asshole, Michelle said, "They have a personality clash. We'll just leave it at that."

"Okay. I call Doctor N. Have a good day. Bye." Out the door he went.

September 11th, 2018, I had a port put in. My neck was a little sore, but nothing I couldn't deal with. When I came home that afternoon, Olivia met me at the door. "Hi, Nana. Did you go to hospital?"

"Yes, I did, honey. Do you want to see what the doctor did to me?"

"Yeah. Let me see."

"Okay, come with me to my bedroom. She followed me and when I pulled back the right side of my V neck sweater, her eyes widened.

"Nana, you've got a big goose basket."

"You mean goose egg."

"No, it's a basket. It'll hold a lot of goose eggs. Does it hurt?"

"Just a little. So you have to be careful when you sit beside me in the recliner. You can't bump my goose basket with your head."

"I'll be careful. I don't want the goose eggs to fall out. If they do you'll have to go back to the hospital and the doctor will have to put them back in." She paused a moment. "Let me see it again." I pulled my sweater to my shoulder. "It's funny looking," she said, followed with a giggle.

"I agree. But it won't always be there. The day will come when the doctor will take it out. It might be a long time, but that's okay. Nana needs it for now."

"Then you keep it for a long time. Will you read me Little Black Sambo?"

"I'll be happy to. But after I read it one time, I need to take a nap."

"Okay. You make it funny 'cause you read it wrong and I have to tell you the right words."

She always read along with me and I'd change the words. I had done the same thing with my children and my other six grandchildren. Most of them

113

liked my version better than what was written. Oliva was the only one who corrected me, but she knew I was doing it on purpose.

Chapter Fourteen

I went back to the cancer center three days later. I had no fear when I took my third infusion. The nurse had the needle in my port, flushed it and drew blood with no problem. I barely felt her stick the needle in. I was so relieved. The four hours didn't seem as long that time, but Michelle and I were glad when it was time to go home. We got our Dr. Pepper to go.

As Michelle and I got into the elevator, we did our count down—"Three down. Five to go."

On the forty mile ride back home I noticed the pain under my rib cage wasn't as intense. When we got home I felt like playing with Olivia. We had a wonderful evening. She loves to play Checkers and Aggravation. We played by her rules. Then we colored and I read books to her. When it was time for her to eat supper, she hugged me and said, "You're the best nana in the whole wide world." My heart melted.

The next morning I got up, drank my breakfast, and realized I had no pain under my rib cage. "Michelle, the chemo is working. After three infusions the ascites has gone down. I want to go outside and enjoy the beauty of the morning."

"Great! I'll fix a cup of coffee and I'll sit with you."

We sat in silence for a few minutes, then I said, "As humans we take so much for granted. Facing a life-threatening disease will sure open your eyes. I see beauty as I've never seen before."

"I'm glad you're enjoying the beauty. I've never been a big nature fan. You always have been. But now that you mentioned it, I do see beauty that I've never paid any attention to."

I walked up and down the hallway several times that day. My strength was coming back. I thanked God with every step I took.

The next morning I wanted to go back outside so I could enjoy the beauty of the morning as the birds were waking up and chirping their sweet music. Michelle helped me get settled on the top step of the front stoop. I glanced to my left and there was a flock of wild turkey strutting across the yard. I got so excited Michelle thought she was going to have to sedate me.

She went back inside to refill our coffee cups. I thought I'd stand for a while. The concrete step was hard on my bony butt. Just as I stood, a bumblebee decided it wanted to land in my hair. I had no idea I could move as fast as I did when the bee dive-bombed me. It came back for seconds and suddenly I was doing a tap dance with a bumblebee.

I looked forward to my mornings sitting outside. Every day I saw more beauty and my heart filled with awe by God's creation.

Michelle enjoyed sitting with me. She was in tune with nature. One morning we were sitting on the top step, sipping coffee. "Mom, do you see those beautiful cardinals? Six are lined up on the roof of the shed."

"Yes, I do! I've never seen that many in one place at the same time. They're awesome!" I took a sip of coffee, then said, "If we sit here long enough do you think the pope will show up?"

Michelle blew coffee through her nose. She coughed and sputtered for a minute. "Are you trying to kill me? I really don't think the pope will show, but damn that was funny. And I think it's time for me to take you back inside."

"Yeah, my bony butt is getting tired. I'll sit in your office chair and look out the window. That fat squirrel is probably wondering where I am."

"Sometime *I* wonder where you are." We laughed as we went back inside.

Later that afternoon, I took a shower and I was strong enough to do it by myself. I was enjoying the feel of water running over my head. I took an extra few minutes and I couldn't remember when water running over my head and body had felt so good. I shampooed, and I felt hair filling my palms as I mas-saged my scalp. I rinsed off the shampoo and my breath caught. Both palms were full of hair and hair was all over the bottom of the tub. "Holy shit! I wasn't expecting that so soon," I said, as if my hair was going to talk back to me.

I towel dried my hair and I was scared to look in the mirror, but I knew I had to get used to going bald. To my surprise, the hair I had lost wasn't that noticeable. However, I was worried about my hair stopping up the bathtub, so after that day I had Michelle help me shampoo it in the kitchen sink. The stopper with holes would let the water go down the drain, but the hairs would stick to it and I hoped it wouldn't stop it up.

Facebook post: "I'm losing my hair but it's a small price to pay for my life. When Michelle blow dries my hair it looks like a snowstorm. We just laugh and make a joke. I refuse to lose my sense of humor."

I thought it was time to explain to Olivia that the medicine I was taking was going to cause me to go bald. I knew it wouldn't be long and she'd notice and I didn't want it to scare her. I told her that soon I'd look like her granddaddy with a bald head. She said, "That'll be funny. When you get bald, I'll draw a smiley face on the back of your head, and you can fool people because they won't know which way you're going."

Facebook post: "As humans we take so much for granted. Facing a life threatening disease will sure open your eyes. I see beauty as I've never seen it before. As the saying goes—take time to smell the roses.

We all get so caught up in the hustle and bustle of life we forget what's really important. I'll never take anything for granted anymore. Not even the breaths I take."

By mid-September, I knew Michelle needed a break. I could see the tired look in her eyes and on her face though she put up a brave front. Mothers know. I told her to take me back to Nameless for a week or two so she could get some rest. She said, "Mom, I don't mind taking care of you. But if you don't mind to go back to Nameless, I could use a break. I'll come back and get you in a week."

We packed a small bag taking only what I thought I'd need for a week. I was sad at the idea of leaving Olivia for a week, but I knew Michelle needed a break.

I have to admit it was good to see my bedroom with pictures of my children, grandchildren, and great-grandchildren, hanging on the walls. And my double bed was so comfortable. I slept on a twin bed at Michelle's. It was comfortable, but I like a double bed with lots of pillows tucked around me. That night I slept like a baby. Though they were in pictures, I felt as if my family was surrounding me.

Being back with Nameless was also a good place to walk. The way the house is built there are three rooms that make a large circle. I walked laps through the rooms, doing all I could to build strength.

The next morning I received a phone call from Michelle. I sweetly answered, "You miss me already!"

"No, Mom. I'm glad you weren't here this morning."

I detected hysteria in her voice and cold chills ran up my spine. "What's wrong, honey?" I held my breath, my heart racing as I wondered if something had happened to Olivia.

"I got up this morning, went into the kitchen to get a cup of coffee and a damn snake was slithering across the floor! I'm so traumatized, I'm not sure I'll ever get over it. You would have dropped dead with a heart attack."

"Holy crap! I would have dropped dead for sure. I'm so sorry, honey. I know it scared you half to death. Is it still in the house?"

"No. I was screaming bloody murder and Marcus came running downstairs. I just pointed because I felt as if I was about to faint. Marcus ran out to the shed, got a hoe, and chopped its head off. He said it was a harmless black snake, but as far as I'm concerned it might as well have been a King Cobra!"

"How did it get inside?"

"Mom, you know there are cracks around the side door that's right off the kitchen. It probably came through there. Marcus is duct taping it now."

"Honey, why don't you pack a few bags and you and Olivia come stay with me until we get colder weather. Snakes are trying to find a warm place."

"That won't work. I'd have to get Olivia up an hour earlier and drive her twenty miles to school every morning, and she'd cry for her daddy if she didn't get to see him when school is out. She's a daddy's girl, you know. She wants her daddy as soon as the last bell rings. I'm stuck right here. Hopefully the side door is where it came in and the duct tape will keep out any more."

"I understand. But you're braver than I am. I'd be moving out!"

"I'll get over it. I'm just glad you weren't here. I'll be there Friday to take you for your chemo."

I dodged a bullet by being back with Nameless. I'm scared of few things, but snakes terrify me.

I also had other pluses by being back with Nameless. My sister, Linda, lives a couple miles from me. Every day she came to check on me. If there was anything I needed, she went to the store and bought it for me. The best part was her bringing me great meals. She's a wonderful cook, and she made sure I ate well. She also cleaned my bathroom, emptied trashcans, changed my bed linen and cleaned the kitchen counter tops. Nameless left a big mess every time he went into the kitchen.

The one week I had planned on staying with Nameless turned out to be a two month stay. However, Michelle was faithful and she took me for chemo infusions every week.

I got up one morning and saw my pillow was covered with white hair. It was falling out more by the day. I went into the bathroom and picked up my hand mirror. I noticed the fine hairs that I call peach fuzz were gone from the sides of my face. I lifted my arms. No pit hair. "Well, it seems like losing hair starts at the top and works its way down. Laws, I know where it's headed next," I said.

I took off my PJ's. They were damp because of the chemo sweats that were plaguing me. I looked at my body in the floor-length mirror on the back of the bathroom door. I couldn't believe what I saw. I had to get to my computer and make my daily post.

Facebook post: "Whooptee-flippin-do! Two months before taking chemo the ascites in my abdominal cavity had me looking like I was nine months pregnant. Now, I'm looking like I'm four months pregnant. I'm so happy. I used to get excited when I took off my clothes. Now, I'm jumping with joy because I can put on clothes. Prayer works! Keep those prayers coming, my sweet friends. I've still got a way to go, but I'm going to make it after all! I'm doing my Mary Tyler Moore imitation, throwing hat into air."

Michelle came for me that Friday and we were on our way to the cancer center. The four hour treatments were rough, so I did my best to joke and laugh. It helped relieve the restlessness. The nurses are used to me acting silly and they seem to enjoy coming into my room to take care of me. That day, every time they change a bag on the IV pole, they asked the same questions. After the third time I said, "You all sure have a short memory. And I'm the one with chemo brain?" And sometimes just to mess with them, I tell them my name was Marilyn Monroe, Demi Moore or Lana Turner. They gave me the stink-eye, but they had a great sense of humor.

That day when it was time to go home, Michelle and I got our Dr. Pepper to go. I filled the Styrofoam cup and pressed the lid down tight. I put a straw in the small hole on the lid and turned it up. Suddenly, I felt something wet running down my PJ top. "Oh, no! My port is leaking. Get a nurse!"

Michelle walked over to me. "Mom, your port is fine. You pressed the lid too tight on the cup and the Dr. Pepper seeped through the other holes in the lid. Jeez!" She took my cup and poured the excess off the lid. "Here. See if this works."

My sweet baby girl put up with me and the crazy things I did and she never complained. She was a trooper. However, I know there were times when she wanted to bop me over the head.

Chapter Fifteen

After five chemo infusions the night sweats were getting worse. I'd wake up during the night and my PJ's would be soaked with sweat. What few hairs I had left were wet and so were my sheets. I'd change PJ's, and towel-dry my hair, but I wasn't in any mood to change my bed three to four times a night. I just switched sides of the bed. By the time I woke up again, the wet side had dried. I'd change PJ's, towel-dry my hair, and get on the side of the bed that was dry enough.

By the first of September, I had chemo itch. I looked like an orangutan as I walked around scratching both sides of my stomach, up and down. At night when I'd go to bed I'd picture it in my mind's eye. It struck me funny. I always found the funny in whatever happened and it got me through the misery.

Every time I took a chemo treatment, as I walked down the long hallways, I'd pass many rooms with people taking infusions. I always smiled and said, "God bless." The smiles I received back were priceless and the patients also gave me a 'God bless'. What was so amazing was the look of surprise in their eyes when I 'God blessed' them. But their sweet smiles let me know how much they appreciated it.

Facebook post: Always give everybody you meet a big smile. You never know who you're going to touch. You can 'God bless' if you want, but a smile is easy and sometimes it means 'God bless' without saying it. Smile on. Show the love. In doing this, it will also make you happy, and happy is healing.

Michelle had faithfully sat through all my treatments with me, but one day I told her to go to the mall, shop, or just walk around. She was suffering with sciatica which she developed while she was pregnant with both her girls. Sitting in the chair in my room was aggravating her condition. She didn't want to leave me, but I assured her I was fine and I was in good hands. She agreed to go.

Before she left, Doctor M came into the room. He had read the notes the nurse had typed in her computer. I knew by the look on his face he wasn't happy. I knew he was going to fuss at me because I had lost weight and I was only eating a few bites of food a day. My taste buds were fried from chemo and I had no appetite. Nameless didn't bother to force food down me. If I said I wasn't hungry, he went his merry way. He wanted to play golf and I could eat or not eat.

Sure enough Doctor M went off. "Why you not eat? Your daughter bad cook?

"She's a terrible cook!"

"What she cook that so bad?"

"Well, one day she cooked chicken, potatoes, and green beans."

"That sound good to me."

"It might have been, but she gave my plate to the dog and I got a bowl of Kibbles and Bits."

His eyes widened and he looked at Michelle. "You feed mama dog food?"

Michelle was holding back a laugh but she shook her head.

"Oh, you be silly. I not believe. It good to have sense of humor, but you tell doctor truth. I come back later. Bye." Out the door he went. He came back later, opened the door just wide enough to stick his head around the frame and said, "Tumor markers go down. Chemo working. Bye." His head disappeared as quickly as if he were dodging a mad dog. I laughed so hard I choked. Michelle had gone by that time and she missed it. His fast *byes* cracked me up every time.

It was also the day a nurse had to attach a Neulasta pump to my stomach. I had to take Neulasta after two treatments the whole time I took infusions. The pump is set to go off sixteen hours after a chemo treatment.

The next evening, I heard the pump beep and I knew the Neulasta was going into my system. It took one hour to empty, then it beeped again and it was time to take it off. I would wrestle with the darn thing, doing my best to pull it loose until my arms wore out. I swore they used super glue to attach it.

The side effects from chemo were bad enough, but they were nothing compared to the side effects of Neulasta. My stomach felt as if somebody had dumped gravel in it. My mouth was dry to the point it felt as if a pail of sand had been dumped in it. The roof of my mouth felt as if it had been coated with polyurethane. My taste buds were dead. Fatigue overtook me. I had to push with all I had just to get out of bed and sit on the sofa. The fatigue usually lasted for three days, then I felt as if I could do a few things.

The next Friday, I was taking my first bag of anti-nausea meds and Doctor M came into my room.

"Your labs are fine. You been eating?"

"Yes, I've been eating. Three times a day my daughter gives me big bowls of Kibbles and Bits."

"Good daughter. Tell her to put gravy on it."

"No problem. She'll mix Gravy Train with it."

"That fine. Eat up. Bye."

I knew he had finally caught on to my humor, which was going to make it more fun for me to keep messing with him.

The cancer center supplied me with Boost Plus. They told me I would have a case waiting for me at the front desk. So, after my infusion I got my Dr. Pepper to go and I was anxious to get out of there. We got out of the elevator and I was hurrying to the front door. Michelle said, "Hold on, Mom. I've got to go to the front desk."

I was a step or two behind her and I said, "Oh, yes. I need my Enfamil."

Michelle shook her head. "That chemo has taken over your brain."

"Well, you know what I meant, Smarty Pants." We laughed.

Note from my journal: September 28th, 2018. I drove my car today! The first time I've been able to drive since May 17th when I picked up Olivia her last day of preschool. It's a beautiful day, almost 70 degrees. I drove around the countryside and the beauty of the trees changing colors was breathtaking. I also went to the cemetery, lay my hand on Mama's headstone and I had a talk with her. She's with me and she's helping me beat the beast that is trying to eat me alive. It's been a blessed day.

The next Friday, I had what I called a dammit day. I got to the cancer center, ready for my last chemo infusion. I was so happy. I'd made it.

Doctor M came into the prep room before the nurse had finished asking all the usual questions. "You have to have four more treatments. Tumor markers not down enough for PET scan. I want your CA-125 count to be thirty-five before you have surgery."

"Dammit! So much for celebrating my last infusion," I said.

Michelle didn't say anything but I could see the look of concern on her face.

The nurse continued with her duties before I would be taken to the room for my infusion. My blood pressure was very low. My white blood count was borderline. I was dehydrated. All the beds were taken and they put me in a recliner, which caused my back muscles to seize. I told the nurse that I couldn't last four hours in a recliner. The nurse said she would get me in a bed as soon as one was available.

I clung to the arms of the recliner, praying I could hold on. Before my first bag of anti-nausea medicine was hung, a nurse came in and said she had a bed for me. "It's the only bed I have and it's nothing like you've had before."

"As long as it's a bed, I don't care," I said.

Michelle and I followed her down a long hallway and we went into a room. The room was the size of a broom closet and my bed was a gurney. I had no call button. The restroom was a long way down the hallway, and I knew I'd have wires and tubes wrapped around the IV pole and probably trip over something, but I was happier on a gurney than I was in a recliner.

I looked at Michelle, "I know this room has to be the cancer center morgue. If an undertaker comes in here don't let them take me."

"I'm going to tell them to tag and bag you. If you protest, I'll tell them not to pay any attention to you because everybody in this center knows what a liar you are."

"Thanks a heap, little darlin'."

We laughed. Then I told her to go to the mall. She didn't have a chair in the tiny room and she couldn't stand for four hours.

"Are you sure you'll be okay? You don't have a call button."

"I'll be fine. I can get off this gurney, unplug my machine and make it to the restroom. I think it's at least a half mile, but I can do it. Stop worrying and just go and have a nice day. And bring me back a present."

"Keep your cell phone handy. If you need me, call and I'll be back as soon as I can."

I held up my cell phone. "I've got it right here. I'll call if I need you. Now go! Have fun."

Just as Michelle left, a nurse came in and hung my first bag. When it was empty the beeper went off. I waited ten minutes and nobody came. I got off the gurney, unplugged my machine and pushed it out into the hallway and just stood there. A nurse saw me and she ran to me. "Can I help you?"

I said, "My beeper has been going off for ten minutes."

Her breath caught in her throat. She said, "I kept hearing a beeper but I couldn't figure out where it was coming from. I'll get you back to bed and I'll get your nurse. She pushed my machine into the room and plugged it in.

Before the nurse came in with my second bag I had to use the restroom. I got off the gurney, hoping I could push the IV pole all the way down the long hallway. The pole had what I called a cock-eyed wheel. No matter which way I tried to push it, it wanted to go another way. I was pushing the pole and I felt something pulling on my port. It scared me for a second. Then I looked back and saw that I had forgotten to unplug the machine. At that moment I began to wonder if maybe Michelle should have stayed with me. However, I unplugged it and I managed to make my way down the long hallway and into the restroom.

I made it back to my room and the nurse was waiting for me so she could hang my second bag. She apologized for not getting to me when my first bag had emptied. "We are swamped today. I'm going as fast as I can, but I'm having a hard time keeping up. I promise I'll be here when this bag is empty."

I said, "Honey, have you had any lunch?"

"No. I don't have time to eat. I'm used to it. I have many days when I don't have time to eat or pee. I just keep going. The patients come first."

"Bless you, sweetie. All of you nurses are angels here on Earth." I picked up a package of cheese crackers I had gotten while I was in the recliner.

"Here, take these. Stuff one in your mouth every chance you have. You need to eat."

"I'll be fine. I want you to eat them. Doctor M will fuss if you don't eat."

"How well I know. But I'm not hungry and you need them. Please take them"

She refused and hurried on her way. I said a prayer for her and all the nurses. When it was time for my chemo bags to be hung, two nurses came into my room to do the verification before they started the drip. I told my main nurse that I was Sam Elliott. She said, "In that case, get ready for a long, wet kiss." The other one said she would kiss me too.

I said, "Okay, I'm not Sam, but I'll take the kisses." Both declined. "Well, I've never been so insulted," I said.

They laughed. My main nurse said, "You're too much, girl. But we get a kick out of you. You make our jobs easier. I wish we had more patients like you."

"I'm glad I can give you a laugh or two. I'm not one to sit on the pity-pot. I find something funny in every situation. There's always a funny side if a person just looks hard enough. Having cancer and fighting for my life is hard, but I'll be laughing and joking until I take my last breath."

They smiled and patted my arm. "Great attitude. Keep us laughing. We love it," said one nurse.

Chapter Sixteen

The chemo was making me weak, but I pushed as hard as I could. I was determined to do what I wanted. I was never going to give up or give in.

Facebook post: October 16th, 2018. As soon as I get the nerve, and I'm working on it, I'm going to post a pic of me wearing my turban, sunglasses, and hoop earrings. It'll be my Lana Turner incognito look.

Facebook post: October 18th, 2018. Hello, my lovies and loonies! It's me. My zippity-doo is gone, but I've still got my da. As the old saying goes, I'm in pretty good condition for the condition I'm in. It's been a rough four months, but I'm going to make it. My spirit is my fate and my spirit is saying, "Hell no! I won't go!" I've lost most of my hair but it's a small price to pay for my life. When my daughters shampoo and blow dry my hair, it looks like a snowstorm. We just laugh and make a joke. I refuse to lose my sense of humor. Olivia, the Tiny Terror is waiting for my bald spot in the back to get big enough for her to draw a smiley face on it.

Facebook post: October 21st, 2018. I'm home and my chemo went well. They jack me on steroids before they give me the chemo which makes me hungry, though I can barely taste food. I'm waiting for my sister, Linda, to bring me a pizza. In the meantime I'm going to chew on the sofa cushion.

Facebook post: October 22nd, 2018. I'm praying that my white blood count stays in the normal range. Thank you for all your prayers and taking this journey with me. You inspire me and give me strength and hope.

While I took my four-hour infusions, I had a lot to time to think and remember. Sometimes old jokes came to mind. This day one surfaced and I laughed as I pictured it in my mind. A cowboy, who just moved to Oklahoma from Texas, walked into a bar and ordered three mugs of Bud. He sat in the back of the room, drinking a sip out of each one in turn. When he finished them, he came back to the bar and ordered three more.

The bartender approached and told the cowboy, "You know, a mug goes flat after I draw it. It would taste better if you bought one at a time."

The cowboy replied, "Well, you see, I have two brothers. One is an Airborne Ranger. The other is a Navy Seal, and both are serving overseas somewhere. When we all left our home in Texas, we promised that we'd drink this way to remember the days when we drank together. So I'm drinking one beer for each of my brothers and one for myself."

The bartender admitted that it was a nice custom, and left it there.

The cowboy became a regular in the bar, and always drank the same way. He ordered three mugs and drank them in turn. One day, he came in and only ordered two mugs. All the regulars took notice and fell silent. When he came back to the bar for the second round, the bartender said, "I don't want to intrude on your grief, but I wanted to offer my condolences for your loss."

The cowboy looked quite puzzled for a moment, then a light dawned in his eyes and he laughed. "Oh, no, everybody's just fine," he explained, "It's just that my wife and I joined the Methodist Church and I had to quit drinking. It hasn't affected my brothers though."

As the hours ticked on by I remembered the night my sister and I went to a fish fry. There were a band and great singers there. I love music. Since places to sit were few when we got there, we took the best seats as close to the front as we could. I sat down by a man. My butt hadn't gotten comfortable in my chair until his mouth went into 4th gear and ran non-stop. He was severely getting on my nerves, but I smiled and tried to be nice. Then a singer began with one of my favorite songs. I wanted to hear the song, not his mouth. I'm straining to hear the song when he said, "You know me and my wife have been married for forty-six years."

I said, "That's nice. I was once married for forty-six minutes. I was in Vegas, got drunk, and married a stranger. As soon as the ceremony was over I caught my flight home. You know what happens in Vegas stays in Vegas, so I left him there!"

"Well, are you still married to him?"

"I have no idea. I don't even remember his name. It doesn't matter, I'll never see him again, and I have no intention of marrying anybody else."

He had nothing to say after that.

The next day after my infusion I was a bit down. I never let myself do that, but for reasons I didn't understand, I felt a case of the blues hitting me. I knew I had to find something positive to fill my mind and chase the demons away. I always say it's the inner demons who want to steal my happy, and I refused to let them take me down.

I went into the bathroom, ran a comb through what little hair I have left, and the comb was full of hair. My eyes teared a bit. Then I said, "Self, there is an upside to this. Find it." Sure enough it came to me. For all you gals who have, or are going through menopause you understand the frustration of the peach fuzz that starts growing on your face, along with wild chin hairs that begin to sprout, and the wild hairs that pop up seemingly overnight above your top lip. For the past twenty years, I was always checking to see if I needed to shave the peach fuzz, grab the tweezers and pluck the wild hairs, and wondering if I got them all before I went outside and the sunshine would show up every hair I had missed.

I felt my face. No peach fuzz. I looked in the magnifying mirror. No chin hairs or upper lip hairs. So, I put on my turban, smiled, waved at myself and said, "Ain't you sumpin'? Cute as a bug in a rug!" I went on with my day with a smile.

Fridays seemed to roll around quickly, but at this time I was glad that time was going by fast. I wanted the nightmare of chemo infusions behind me. Michelle picked me up the next Friday and I put on my turban. I kept it on during the four hours of infusions. It was making my head itch and I wanted to take it off, but my vanity, what little I had left wouldn't let me. When it was time to head home that day, I got my Dr. Pepper to go.

Michelle was driving down the street and I said, "This turban is driving me crazy. It's hot, my head itches, and my ears are mashed too close to my head." I reached up and flipped my ears out. I looked like Dumbo, ready for takeoff. As she passed cars I looked over at the drivers and flipped my ears back and forth. I got some strange looks and a few laughs. At least I had made somebody laugh who might have been having a bad day and needed cheering up.

"Mom, why don't you get some red bandanas and sport a do-rag? And wear big hoop earrings. I think it would look smashing."

"You might be onto something. I'll think about it," I said.

Chapter Seventeen

October arrived, my favorite month of the year. I was anxious to drive out to the countryside when the leaves started changing colors. I was starting to feel weak again, and my energy level had dropped. But I pushed on.

Many people had warned me about chemo brain and how it erases a person's memory. I was already forgetful, and I was worried. However, as the weeks passed, I seemed to be holding it together. Until one night. It was time for me to take my anti-nausea pill. I kept all my meds on top of my dresser. I took the pill out of the bottle, then realized I didn't have any water. I went into the kitchen and got a bottle of water out of the fridge. I came back to my bedroom, picked up my pill and before I opened the bottle of water, I looked straight ahead. There on the nightstand was another full bottle of cold water. I had no memory of getting it out of the fridge. I think a fairy put it there just to mess with my head. Surely.

A couple days later, I went into the bathroom. I brushed my teeth, then my bladder reminded me that I had come into the bathroom to pee. I had already brushed my teeth. I did my business and headed into the kitchen, hoping I'd remember the water was in the fridge instead of the oven.

I had been cooking a few meals, but it was becoming a task as my strength was waning. As much as I don't like a kitchen and as much as I don't like to cook, I was wishing I had the strength to do it, and if I did, I knew I'd cook all day long. It's astounding how your likes and dislikes change when you aren't able to do anything. You miss not being able to do the simple things you once took for granted. You see the world through different eyes. You see more beauty, which is great.

I admire the beauty around me and I continued to pray that the day would come when I could once again take a walk through the woods and enjoy nature. Minus the snakes.

Facebook post: October 18th, 2018. Enjoy every minute the Good Lord gives you, even the minutes that are aggravating and stressful because when those moments are taken from you, you'll wish you had them plaguing you.

One day my sister, Linda, brought me a huge container of mashed potatoes. My taste buds were fried, but I craved potatoes. She had cooked at least three pounds. I'm sure I ate at least one pound. I thought I might be able to eat another large bowl of potatoes before I went to bed. Linda is doing her best to fatten me up. I was hoping it would put a pound or two on my bony butt. Doctor M and the nurses at the cancer center kept telling me to eat a diet high in carbs. I was eating carbs and all the stuff they told me to eat, but so far the scales haven't moved.

The chemo brain saga continued. I had words in my head but when they came out of my mouth, it wasn't what I meant to say. I was having a conversation with my daughter. In my head I had the word incapacitated. When it came out of my mouth it was decapitated. I laughed so hard when I heard myself say it, I hurt all over.

Michelle bent over double. She said, "Well, if you were decapitated I think that would render you incapacitated."

Olivia was antsy because her mother and I were talking. She wanted to play Sorry. I told her I would play, but if she lost and cried about it I wasn't going to. She said she wouldn't. Michelle said she would play with us.

Michelle won the game and Olivia teared up. She said, "Nana, get me a tissue."

I got a tissue and wiped her eyes and nose. "You said you wouldn't cry if you lost, but you did. You're a sore loser."

"I'm not sore. I don't hurt anywhere. I'm sad," she said.

"Well, you can't win every game. When I win or Mommy wins, you're supposed to clap and be happy for us. When you win, we clap and say, 'Yay, Olivia.'"

After her meltdown, she wanted us to play another game with her. She was determined to win. She seemed to be in deep thought as Michelle set up the game board. She said, "If Mama wins and Nana wins and I win, then Nameless will be the loser."

Michelle said, "Nameless isn't playing, but if he was and he lost what should we do if he cries?"

Without missing a beat, Olivia said, "We'll give him a tissue! Let's play!"

By Halloween, I was losing strength, fast. I pushed with all I had, every day. I didn't have the energy to hand out candy to the Trick-or-Treaters. I could see them standing outside when Nameless opened the door and handed them candy. They were so precious and they warmed my heart as I remembered all the Halloweens that I had taken my three children, and my six oldest grandchildren around the neighborhood, and they came home with big sacks of candy and I'd steal all the Snickers.

November arrived with a vengeance. It was colder than usual for the first week. I was waiting for Michelle to pick me up and head to Owensboro for a treatment. I looked out the window. It was what at one time I would have called a rainy, gloomy day, and it would have sent me into depression. Not anymore. The rain was beautiful. I saw no gloom. I was happy to be alive and that made it a beautiful day. I was still amazed at how I viewed the world since I was diagnosed. I saw beauty in everything and everywhere.

Snow covered the grounds on the 9th. We usually don't get snow until late December. I began to wonder if Mother Nature needed a new GPS.

Note from my journal: November 9th, 2018. For six months, everybody complained about the heat. Now they complain about the cold and snow. Not me. I don't care what the temp is or what it is doing outside. I'm just glad to be alive. Once you face death, your perspective about everything changes. I only see the beauty. I admit if we have to drive through a blizzard so I can take my chemo, I might change my tune.

Facebook post: November 10nd, 2018. Many times I've asked for prayers for me and healing. Today, I'd like to ask for prayers for my caregiver, my daughter Michelle. This journey has been hard on her. She makes the forty mile drive every Friday so I can take my chemo treatments. Never once has she complained. I see the tiredness in her eyes and my heart hurts. I pray that God will continue to give her strength. We've still got a way to go.

Two days before I had to make the forty mile trip for my next chemo treatment, it snowed. The snow was beautiful, but I was concerned about the roads being slick. I woke up that morning to make the long trip. Snow was still on the ground but it didn't look too bad. We took blankets, water, food and a coffee can for me to pee in just in case something happened and we were stuck on the roads.

The roads were clear and the sun was shining through the car windows. We didn't need the heater. I checked into the cancer center and they were not packed and rushed. A nurse stuck the needle into my port so she could draw blood. She couldn't get it. The nurse told me to turn my head as far to the left as I could. I did, but it still didn't work. She told me to scoot to the edge of my chair and put my head as close to my knees as I could. It didn't work. She told me to keep my head down and put my left arm around my neck. It didn't work. She told me to keep my head down and put my right arm around my neck. It didn't work. She said, "I'm going to try one more thing. I'm going to put you in the upside down chair." When she said upside down, she wasn't kidding. I was on my head.

"Hang on, here goes," she said, and she inserted the needle.

I said, "Gee, my legs haven't been this high over my head for years!"

Nurse started laughing and she almost dropped the blood tube. "Will you shut up? I can't do my job." I kept my mouth shut and she said, "Bingo. The blood is coming. I've got to fill four tubes. Don't move, I don't want it to stop before I get all I need."

I said a silent prayer, *Please, God. Let my blood flow.*

She filled the tubes, then set me upright. I didn't dare move. All my blood had gone to my head and I was dizzy. By the time she had the tubes labeled, I was fine and ready to go to my room.

Note from my journal: November 10th, 2018. I know people mean well, but there are times when I'm asked questions that I take offense to. When I'm asked if I've given much thought to the Hereafter, as if I'm on my death bed, I always give the answer my mamaw used to say. "Yes. Every time I go from one room to the other, I ask myself, 'what am I here after'." I don't like to be questioned about my faith or what I believe. When I am, then I become a smart butt.

Chapter Eighteen

Note from my journal: November 11th, 2018.   My chemo brain is at work today. I sat down at the old piano and I could barely remember a key past Middle C. I couldn't remember the flats and sharps. I gave it up and decided to get out my great-grandpa's fiddle. I blew off the dust and thought for a few minutes. I couldn't remember if I was supposed to run the bow over the fiddle or the fiddle over the bow. So, I thought I'd just sing. The words were in front of me as I opened up the hymn book. I started singing and the neighbor's dogs started howling. I took it as a sign that they were enjoying it.

Olivia likes to play the old piano too. It's in bad need of tuning, but to her it sounds fine. I have a small wooden cross sitting on top of it. She picked it up, hugged it to her heart and said, "Nana, God and Jesus are going to make you well."

My eyes leaked as I said, "Yes, honey, they will."

Note from my journal: November 13th, 2018. I just shampooed and watched what little hair I had left slide down the drain. I admit I teared up. Then I jerked my butt back into gear and counted my blessings. I'm still alive. Cancer and chemo can take the beauty of my hair, but they can't take the beauty of my soul. I'm old. I'm bald. I'm beautiful.

Note from my journal: November 15th, 2018. Snow is still coming down. I love to watch the flakes fall. The icicles hanging on the trees and railing of the deck is so pretty. I may not think it's all that pretty tomorrow when I have to make the forty mile trip to get my chemo, but make it I will, and I'll enjoy the beauty from inside a warm car.

Note from my journal: November 16th, 2018. I've got a small Christmas tree, the perfect size for the coffee table. I'm going to get it out of the attic, and Olivia and I are going to draw turkeys on construction paper, cut them out and hang them on the branches. The turkeys might look like cats when we finish, but we know what they are. Let the holidays begin!

Facebook post: November 22nd, 2018. I'm reading all the posts and seeing the pictures of families together and preparing for a big Thanksgiving dinner. My heart fills with joy and happiness for all of you. My heart is a little sad because I had high hopes that I would be strong enough by now to take Olivia to the kitchen and bake pies, make cookies, or whatever she wants to cook. It isn't going happen. I'm getting weaker by the day. But if the Good Lord is willing, I'll be well and the cancer will be behind me next year. If so, then I'm going to take her out into the woods and we're going to chase wild turkeys and pardon them. Happy Thanksgiving.

As November passed, I was weaker and I spent more time in bed. As I lay, praying for healing, my mind would wander back in time and I'd remember the things I did when I was in grade school and how I drove the teachers crazy. My memories always made me laugh. Since laughter is good medicine, I was glad I still had clarity of years gone by.

I was in fifth grade, and gum chewing wasn't allowed. But, me being me, I was going to chew gum. I thought I was slick enough to pull it off. A few times I did. One day the teacher walked over to my desk and said, "Take the gum out of your mouth and stick it on the end of your nose."

I did. Then I started giggling as I pictured in my mind what a wad of gum must look like on the end of my nose. I giggled and couldn't shut up, which had the whole class giggling. So, the teacher told me to go stand in the hallway. I did, but I was still giggling and she could hear me.

She opened the classroom door and told me to go to the principal's office. Off I went. I walked into his office, and I'll never forget the look on his face. He said, "What in the world? Why is there gum on the end of your nose?"

I said, "Because Mrs. S won't let me put it in my mouth."

He said, "Throw it in the trash can and go back to class."

I threw it into the trash can, but I really wanted to keep it on the end of my nose and go back to my classroom. I could tell that he was holding back a laugh.

I walked back into my classroom, and all the students laughed. I laughed with them. I laughed harder when I saw Mrs. S's face turn red. She was sure the principal would deal harsh punishment for me. I'm surprised he didn't. I think he had more important things on his mind at the time.

The next day I was napping and my sister delivered a big teddy bear that a friend had bought me. It was twice my size and probably weighed as much as I do. I woke up, walked into the living room, still half asleep, and I saw this monster sitting in the recliner. I jumped, screamed, and if I had been close to my gun I would have shot it.

I laughed as I visualized the police busting through the front door because a neighbor had called 911 and reported gunshots. My mind's eye could see the look on their faces, guns drawn, only to find that a crazy ol' lady of seventy-six had shot and blown a teddy bear to smithereens.

I was sleeping more and acid reflux plagued me. I'd wake up several times a night with the taste of vomit in my mouth. I took acid reducers and it helped, but it didn't completely stop. After I'd take a pill, hoping my stomach would settle down, I'd be awake and my mind would spin as I recalled things from my past.

This memory came to my head one night. It was 1978 and I was living in Florida. A neighbor was a Mary Kay cosmetic saleswoman. She begged me to come to one of her meetings, or pep rally, as I called them. I agreed to attend. The rally was being held in a big room she had rented and there were a lot of ladies there. She was up front going through her spiel, telling us how we could make big money and even win a pink Cadillac. She was jumping around like a Mexican jumping bean, and all the ladies were clapping and jumping up and down, all excited about the get rich fast speech they were buying into.

I knew it was a load of crap. The more she talked the more irritated I became. She was hyping the ladies up just so she could recruit them, and she'd make money from each of them when they made sales. I made myself sit through the whole thing while I gritted my teeth.

After the meeting was over, the leader of the pack, as I called her, walked up to me. She said the following week that several cosmetic companies were hosting a beauty contest in Tampa, and she wanted me to represent Mary Kay. The whole idea struck me as funny, so me being me, I said sure.

The night of the contest I grabbed a dress out of my closet. Nothing fancy. I put on my high heels to match and I was ready. The 'leader of the pack' picked me up. There were twelve contestants, all younger than me and very pretty. I thought it would be funny when I came in dead last as I knew I would. I won't go into detail on all I had to do and the questions I had to answer when the MC stuck a microphone in my face.

We had to wait thirty minutes for the judges to decide. Finally, all of us went back on stage. The name of the 3rd runner up was called. I had her picked out. The name of the 2nd runner up was called. I had her picked out, too.

"And the winner is"—long pause. I had the winner picked out.

My name was called. I froze. I looked out into the audience and the 'leader of the pack' was motioning for me to step forward. A lady placed a tiara on my head, handed me a dozen silk roses, and the MC slipped a pretty dinner ring on my finger. I was handed a big trophy with the engraving 'Miss Glow Girl'.

It was time for me to take my stroll down the small walkway and smile as flash bulbs blinded me. I was dying laughing inside. I was Miss Glow Girl, representing Mary Kay, and I was wearing Max Factor makeup. My children called me Miss Glow Worm. To this day we still laugh about it.

Chapter Nineteen

Thanksgiving day, my sister, Linda, had cooked a big meal for her family. I was too weak and too sick to go, but she brought me a plate with all the traditional dishes I had always loved. I propped up in bed, and took one bite of everything she had on the plate. My taste buds were dead, I was nauseous, and each bite felt as if rocks were hitting my stomach.

I continued to get weaker by the day. It was all I could do to roll out of bed, get to the bathroom and back. A few times I made it into the kitchen and got a bottle of water. Again, I'd lost control of my bladder and bowels. I couldn't figure out what was happening. When I first started taking chemo infusions, I gained strength, the pain under my rib cage disappeared, and I thought the chemo was working wonders. At this point it seemed to be doing a reverse.

I was still writing in my journal and at times I'd posted on Facebook. I pushed with all I had to do these two simple things. I was determined I wouldn't give in or give up, though the fight became harder by the day.

Note from my journal. November 28th, 2018. My seventh grandbaby, Olivia, came into my life when I was seventy-plus. She gave me a new lease on life. Now, a short five years later, I'm fighting with all my soul and climbing the highest mountain I've ever had to climb just to stay around for a few more years. There is no way that God sent her to me just to take me away so soon. For you, my precious Olivia, I'll keep fighting. We've got a lot more memories to make. You are my fuel.

Lying in bed, my mind kept spinning, remembering. I think it was my defense mechanism to keep my mind off what was happening to my body at that time. This memory came to mind. It was two years ago.

I came out of K-Mart and there was a young girl standing between her car and mine, talking on her cell phone.

"I don't know what to do. I locked my car and went into K-Mart. I came out and I've pushed the button on my key a dozen times. It won't unlock. I can't afford to call a locksmith and I have to be at work in thirty minutes."

I walked over to her. "I think I can help. Do you see the round metal thing beside the door handle?"

"Yeah."

"Push up on it."

She pushed it up. "Insert your key, then turn it."

"I heard it unlock!"

"Yeah, works every time. It'll do the same thing with your trunk.

Wide-eyed, she said, "I didn't know!"

"See, it always pays to have an old lady around. The same old ladies that you youngins don't think know shit from apple butter."

She was so happy she was in tears. I walked off while she finished her conversation on her cell phone.

Note from my journal: November 29th, 2018. I'm watching the snow fall outside and it's so pretty. Suddenly, I looked down and thought, *it's snowing inside, too*. It was hair falling out in my lap. Chemo, oh chemo, how do I hate thee—let me count the ways.

Snowflakes were falling and I was reminiscing as I looked at the beauty through my bedroom window. I was remembering when we first moved to Missouri in 1976. The dialect in Missouri takes some getting used to, and it took me a spell to understand a lot. The first day we were there, I hadn't had time to grocery shop.

We went into a little cafe and my oldest daughter, Cathye, ordered a 7-Up. The waitress said, "We ain't got no wite sodie."

Cathye gave me a puzzled look.

I said, "No white soda. Just order a Coke."

She ordered a Coke. The waitress said, "Ye want it in a bottle or in a glass over ize."

I quickly said, "Bottle is fine."

After we ate I went to a gas station. In the mid 70's they still had full service gas stations. I pulled up to the pump and the attendant came out. I rolled down my window and said, "Fill it up."

He said, "Ye want I should check yer earl?"

I said, "My what?"

He said, "Under yer hood. Yer earl."

I said, "Sure. If you find Earl under there, please drag him out."

I got a strange look, but he opened the hood, pulled out the dipstick, wiped it, then put it back in. He pulled it out the second time and walked over to me. "The level is fine but it's dirty. You want I should drain it and put fresh in?"

"No, I don't have time today. I'll come back later and get my earl changed."

We were still laughing as I pulled out of the lot. We had learned two words in the boot heel of Missouri language. Sodie was soda, and earl was oil.

November 30th, Michelle picked me up and we headed to Owensboro for my tenth infusion. I was so weak, it was all I could do to sit upright and make the trip. I wanted to lay my head against the window, but I was determined not to give in.

When we arrived at the cancer center, Michelle had to steady me, but I managed to walk into the building. I clung to the rail of the elevator as Michelle pushed the button for the second floor. With her help I made it to the waiting room. The receptionist put on my wristband and I took a seat, praying I wouldn't have to wait very long. I just wanted to get into a bed. My head felt as if it weighed fifty pounds, and I was having a hard time holding it upright.

Before the nurse could ask all the questions in what I'd always called the interrogation room, Doctor M came in. I explained to him how badly the last treatment had taken me down and I could barely get out of bed. I asked if he had increased my dosage.

His eyes widened and he said, "No. Same dosage. Doctor don't lie."

I said, "I didn't say you lied, I just thought you might have sneaked one in on me."

As he did a quick turn to leave, he said, "Doctor don't sneak!"

I didn't even get one of his fast 'byes'.

Again, I had to almost stand on my head so the RN could get blood from my port. But she got it. I was taken to a private room with a restroom. I couldn't wait to get into the welcoming bed.

The nurse hung my first bag of anti-nausea meds. All I wanted to do was sleep. Before I could doze off, Doctor M came into my room. "Your white blood count is good. But I read what you told the nurse. Your body is too old to tolerate chemo. This is your last infusion. I'm going to order you a PET scan. We'll see where you stand. Your CA-125 is sixty-nine. It bumped up nine points. I wanted the chemo to get your numbers down to the thirties, but don't think it's going to happen. You get a call when you get appointment. Bye."

I was so relieved. Doctor M finally realized that I was back to what I called ground-zero. I was as sick, if not sicker, than when I first began with chemo infusions. I knew the chemo was killing me faster than cancer. It was a long day and I was anxious to go home and get into my comfortable bed. I didn't want my Dr. Pepper to go.

Michelle steadied me and I had the strength to make it to the car. I could see the worried look in her eyes, but she didn't say anything. I patted her arm. "Mama is going to be fine, honey. No more chemo. I'll get my strength back."

"I'm glad he finally realized that the chemo was killing you. I didn't say anything because I knew you would stop the treatments when you thought it was time."

"I think I should have stopped them after my sixth infusion. That's when I started going downhill, but I wanted to hang on and let the chemo kill this cancer. We'll just have to pray harder."

"I don't think we can pray any harder, but we'll continue praying and believing. I admire your spunk and determination. You always were a hardhead."

We laughed. Being a hardhead was in my favor at that point in my life.

When we reached the lobby Michelle noticed a sign on the front desk. 'Free caps.' "Mom, do you want a cap? They're free and it will keep your bald head warm."

"Sure." I looked through the pile. I picked out a pink and purple interwoven one. I put it on my head and it came down to my chin. "I'll have to cut out eye holes. I can't see through this thing."

"Give it here," she said as she pulled it off my head. She rolled it up, tucked it here and there and stuck it back on my head.

"Well what do you know? I can see and it isn't tight and it doesn't smash my ears to my head."

"Ya don't say."

"Oh, you can be such smart butt. But thanks. It does feel good and it'll keep my head warm."

The forty mile trip back home seemed more like four hundred, but I hung on. Before we made it back to Nameless, Michelle said, "Mom, give me a few days to rearrange things in your bedroom at my house. Since you've been gone, Olivia and I set up camp in there. I'm taking you back home with me."

"Oh, thank you, honey. I don't want to be a burden and wear you out again, but it sure will be nice to come back. I've missed Olivia so much."

"I would have brought you sooner, but you were too scared of snakes coming into the house. It's cold enough that all the snakes have found a bed for the winter. We haven't seen another one. I think we're safe. And you're not a burden. You're back to being helpless and Nameless can't take care of you and Aunt Linda can't be with you around the clock."

"Nameless tries, but he doesn't know what to do."

"I know he does, but trying isn't good enough. It has to be done, and due to circumstance, I'm the only one to do it. Besides, Olivia will be happy to see you every day. I didn't realize how sick you are again. You didn't tell me everything you told the nurse."

"No, I didn't. I didn't want to put more worry and stress on you. But you know now, and I'm so thankful that you're willing to take me back in."

"I'm your daughter. I'll never forsake you! You should know that!"

I wiped my eyes. "I know. Sometimes it's hard to swallow my pride."

"Pride goeth before the fall. So, shaddup, as you're always telling me. I'm in charge now."

"Yes ma'am, your honor!" We laughed. My heart was doing a tap dance.

Chapter Twenty

My PET scan was scheduled for December 7th, 2018. I was happy that I was getting it done so quickly, and a bit anxious about the results. I prayed with all my soul the scan would show that my tumor in my left ovary had shrunk to the size of a mustard seed. If it had, then I would be ready for surgery. I also had an appointment to see my gynecologist on December 10th, 2018. She would do my surgery if she thought I was strong enough. I prayed that I would be.

December the 3rd, 2018. My bed was getting too comfortable and I knew I had to push harder. I was sitting up more and walking around three rooms that made a circle. Five laps around the rooms were all I could do, but I knew it would help build my strength. I was sitting on the sofa when the doorbell rang. Nameless went to the door. "Come in," he said.

I recognized the voices. My oldest daughter, Cathye, and my oldest granddaughter, Christina, had come for a visit. It was a gray, gloomy day. No sunshine was a bit depressing, but my daughter and granddaughter were my sunshine.

They sat down on the sofa beside me and we had a chit-chat for a few minutes. Christina said, "Granny, is it okay if we lay hands on you and pray over you?"

"Well, of course. I need all the prayers I can get. Let me get back in bed."

Cathye assisted me into the bedroom. I couldn't get into my high bed without a little stepstool. I attempted to make the steps, but I was unsteady. Christina boosted me with no effort and I fell on the bed. I laughed. "Well, that's one way of doing it."

Cathye fluffed my pillow and neatly tucked it under my head. Then she put a pillow under my knees. I lay prone, and closed my eyes. Cathye was on the left side of my bed, holding my hand. Christina was on the right side, holding my hand. First she began rebuking the devil. She placed her right hand on my abdomen. She spoke in a furious voice and she rebuked to the point she almost scared me. I was praying she had scared the devil, too. After she rebuked, she kept her hand on my abdomen and began to pray aloud. As she continued to pray, she ran her hand over my body from head to toe.

I had my eyes closed, repeating her words in my head. As I've said, this was a dark gloomy day and the sun hadn't peeked through the clouds once. As she was praying, suddenly the sun lit up my bedroom, and my daughter and granddaughter saw my body light up from head to toe. It was as if I was totally bathed in the light of God. It only lasted a few seconds, then the sun was gone.

I had my eyes closed and I couldn't see my body, but I did feel the warmth of the sun. They told me what had happened. I said, "My body lit up with brightness from the love of God." It was at that moment I believed I was healed.

Some will laugh or scoff at this story. Some will believe. It makes no difference to me. When I write or when I'm talking with someone, I always say, "Take what you want and leave the rest." The same applies here.

Facebook post: December 4th, 2018. If you have a few minutes for me, I really need prayers. This Friday I have another PET scan done. I'm praying with all my soul that it will show the tumor in my ovary has shrunk to the size of a mustard seed and all the ascites is gone. It'll be my Christmas miracle. Your prayers and well wishes have gotten me this far. Thank you from the bottom of my heart.

December 6th, 2018, I had just gotten out of bed and poured myself a cup of coffee when Michelle rang the doorbell. I opened the door. "Come in, honey."

"I'm here to pack your two suitcases. You're going home with me."

"Oh, thank you, honey. Let's get packed. I can't wait to get out of here."

"Where's Nameless?"

"He's out on the deck, smoking a cigar and reading the paper."

"You sit down. I know where your things are and I know what you need to take. Did Nameless take your cases to the attic?"

"Are you kidding? They're in the garage. It took him a week to take them out of the kitchen. If I hadn't pitched a fit, they'd still be there."

"I'll go to the garage, get them and I'll have you packed in no time. Just rest."

I sat down on the sofa and drank my coffee. Michelle had everything packed in less than thirty minutes. She carried the suitcases out to her car, then she came back inside for me. "Put your heavy terry-cloth robe on. It's cold out there."

My robe was hanging over the armrest of the sofa. I picked it up and Michelle held it while I stuck my arms into the long, warm sleeves. "Are you going to tell Nameless bye?"

"Yeah, I'll stick my head out the backdoor and tell him."

Before I could make it to the backdoor, Nameless came inside. "Are you leaving?"

"Yes, Michelle has me packed. I'm not good with goodbyes, so I'll—"

Before I could finish my sentence, he hugged me and said, "Goodbye isn't necessary. I'll be out to see you at least twice a week. If you need anything before I come, just call me."

I was happy to be going home with Michelle, but I felt a knot forming in my throat. Nameless had been so good to me for the past twelve years, and I appreciated him with all my heart. I knew I could always count on him. I squeezed his hand, but no words would come out. He assisted me to the car. "I'll see you soon," he said, and closed the car door.

The twenty mile trip to Michelle's seemed as if it were only two miles. I had my happy back. I was comfortable with Nameless, but my happy was missing. I knew it was important for my healing to feel happy.

When we arrived I was getting tired, but my happiness gave me strength that had also been missing. Michelle assisted me into the house. She settled me in bed, then unpacked my two suitcases. I dozed off while she was busy putting my things in drawers and the closet.

She gently shook my shoulder. "Mom, you need to eat breakfast. I'll scramble you two eggs and fix toast if you think you can eat it. I'll brew another pot of coffee. I could use a cup myself."

"That sounds good. I think my taste buds are coming back to life and it's just been a week since I stopped the chemo. And I'm also gaining strength."

I ate breakfast and what little I could taste was great. I took my plate to the kitchen, rinsed it off and placed it in the sink.

"Mom, Marcus and I put the lights on the Christmas tree yesterday. Do you want to watch me decorate it? I need to get it done before Olivia comes home from school. She'll be picking up ornaments, dropping them and breaking them. You know I'm particular about my tree being decorated, just so. She'll also rearrange every ornament unless I keep a close eye on her."

"I'd like that very much. Let me pour me a cup of coffee and I'll join you in the living room." While I was pouring my coffee, Michelle turned on the radio and Christmas carols were playing in the background. The beautiful music helped me get into the Christmas spirit. I missed the days when my children and grandchildren had helped me decorate a tree, and we baked goodies for the holiday. It seemed as if it were only yesterday in one way, and it seemed as if it had been many years ago in another.

I sipped my coffee as I sat in the comfortable overstuffed chair. As I watched her decorate, many Christmases past went through my mind. I fought tears as I wondered from time to time if this would be my last Christmas. I pushed the negative thoughts from my head and replaced them with visions of many Christmases to come. God was going to heal me. I had to keep praying and believing. I knew if I let the devil put negative thoughts in my head he would win. No way was I going to let that happen. I silently prayed as I listened to the music, *Dear God, please heal me and let me have many more Christmases to celebrate the birth of your Son, Jesus Christ.*

The decorating was done. Michelle plugged in the lights. My eyes widened as if I were a child seeing my first Christmas tree. "It's beautiful. I just want to sit here and admire it. But I need to exercise. I'm going to go up and down the ten basement steps. I can't just sit and lie. I've got to build my strength so I'll be strong enough for surgery when we get the call."

"Okay, but I'm going in front of you on the way down and I'll be behind you on the way back up. The last thing you need is to fall up or down the steps. Olivia will be home soon, so let's get it done."

Going down was easy. Coming back up was a struggle. With every step I kept saying, "Come on, ol' gal. You can do this." I made it back to the top. I was proud of myself, but I was exhausted. "I couldn't have done this a week ago. I'm getting stronger. I'll continue to get stronger by the day. I won't give up."

"You're a fighter, Mom. You always have been. You wouldn't have made it through life this far if you didn't have a fighting spirit."

"Fight should have been my middle name," I said. Michelle agreed.

I lay down and I was asleep by the time my head hit the pillow. I woke up when I heard Olivia's voice and I heard her footsteps running toward my bedroom. She opened my bedroom door, and yelled, "Hi, Nana! You came back home! I had a good day at school, and the teacher gave me a yellow sticker.

That's the best color you can get when you pay attention."

"That's awesome, sweet pea. Nana is proud of you. Do you want to give Nana a hug?"

"Are you going to stay in bed with your eyes closed?"

"I might for a little while, but when I get up I'll play cards with you. Please give Nana a hug."

She didn't say a word. She turned and left the room. I listened to her footsteps running away from me. To her I was once again a sick old lady in bed. Her fun Nana was gone. I held back my tears. I understood, but it broke my heart. When I had left her and gone back with Nameless, I had reached the point where I could play with her. Now, I was back to being in bed and almost helpless.

Chapter Twenty-One

Michelle had potato soup cooking in the crockpot. The smell made my tummy growl. She filled a bowl and brought it to me. I wolfed it down. I was still a bit nauseous, but I was able to hold food down. A great improvement.

Olivia came into my room. "Nana, I decorated my Christmas tree in my room, do you want to see it?"

"I sure do, honey." I stood up and I felt stronger. I followed her into her bedroom. "My goodness. That's the prettiest tree I've ever seen. Did you do that all by yourself?"

"Yeah. Mommy said I can't touch the big tree that she decorated."

"Well, you have your own tree and it's perfect. Do you want to play cards?"

"Yes! I'll get them. Can we play at the card table in the TV room?"

"Nana will give it a try." We played two games of War, then I had to lie down.

That night, she came into my bedroom with Michelle, and she tucked the covers under my chin and around my sides.

"Are you making a burrito out of Nana?"

"Yeah. And I'll turn out your lamp. If you need anything just yell. Mommy will take care of you. I have to sleep 'cause I've got to go to school tomorrow."

"Goodnight, sweetie. I'll see you tomorrow when you come home from school." I lay in darkness and my tears flowed. "Dear God, please heal me and give me another ten years with my baby girl." Peace filled my heart and I fell into a deep sleep.

The next day I went for my PET scan. I had a new nurse because she works in what I called the nuke department. She couldn't use my port to inject me with the radioactive iodine. She did find a vein that didn't blow. After she injected me with iodine, she took me to a room with a recliner. I had to wait an hour before the tech could do the scan.

She stayed with me for a few minutes, making sure I was comfortable. She brought me a warm blanket and a cup of ice chips. I had to be NPO for the procedure with the exception of water. I had continuous dry mouth from chemo, and I was thankful for water and ice chips.

Nurse said, "Your daughter is so sweet and she's so pretty. Well dressed and groomed to perfection."

I said, "Yeah," with a deep sigh. "I don't see why she can't act like the white trash that I raised her to be."

Nurse shook her head and said, "I know what you mean. Children can be such a disappointment."

We both had a good laugh. I was glad somebody not only understood my sense of humor, but she had one to match mine.

An hour later I was taken to what I called the torture tunnel. I had to lay flat on my back, both arms over my head, and I wasn't supposed to move a muscle for thirty minutes. My arms were trembling, and my back felt as if it had snapped in half, but I managed to hold on. The tech told me that my gynecologist would have results by Monday.

Monday, December 10th, 2019, Michelle took me to Owensboro. I was so anxious to get the results of my PET scan. The forty mile trip was a snap. I had gained strength in the past ten days since I had my last chemo infusion, and the excitement had my adrenaline pumping. I knew in my heart that I was going to receive good news.

We arrived at Doctor A's office on time. Michelle signed me in. We waited twenty minutes and a nurse called my name. She took me to Doctor A's consultation room. We waited another twenty minutes, and I was like an antsy child. I couldn't sit still. I was wearing Michelle out, but I couldn't contain myself.

Doctor A came into the room and she had a big smile. She sat down behind her desk and said, "Well, you sure look a lot better than the first time I saw you. You were knocking on death's door. The chemo worked. I think you'll be happy to hear that your PET scan showed no signs of malignance. It's as if you never had cancer."

I couldn't hold back my tears of joy. I managed to say, "I got my Christmas miracle! I knew I would."

Doctor A said, "It sure looks that way. I couldn't be happier for you." She paused a minute. "I can do your surgery. I've removed cancerous ovaries for over twenty years—"

I was so excited, I interrupted. "How soon can you get me scheduled?"

"Hold on a minute. I have a colleague who practices in Evansville. He's had four more years of school, and more practice in your kind of surgery. It's his specialty. He's also an oncologist. You'll be in good hands with him if you have no objections."

"I have no objections. I'll take your recommendation." I looked at Michelle, and she nodded her head, letting me know that she was with me in having my surgery done by a doctor who specialized in the kind of surgery that I needed.

"I'll give him a call and his office will call you when he has an opening for a consultation. He's a busy man and it might take longer than you want, but you'll have more time to gain strength. We want you as strong and healthy as possible. This is a serious operation and you'll be down for six weeks."

"Six weeks is nothing compared to what I've been through," I said.

"I can't stress the importance of eating. You need to eat at least six to eight meals a day. I know you're not a big eater by your size, but you need to put as much weight on as you possibly can before your surgery. And you need to stay in motion. Walking is the best, but it's cold outside, so just walk through the house."

"I'll do my best to eat more. I have a small stomach and it doesn't take much to fill me up. However, my taste buds are coming back to life and my daughter is a great cook. I'll eat something every two hours. I walked up and down ten steps yesterday. I'll keep doing it and I'll up my trips as fast as I can."

"Up and down steps is the best exorcise. Keep it up and add a trip every day." She rose from her chair and walked around her desk just as I stood up. She patted my back and said, "God bless."

"Thank you. God bless you, too." I was choking on tears of joy and my eyes leaked as I talked.

Michelle and I walked out of the office and tears of joy were still running down my face. Before we reached the car I thrust my fist into the air and did my best imitation of Tyler Perry's character, Madia. I yelled, "Hallelujer! Praise the Lort!"

We got into the car. I rolled down the window and yelled, "Hey, devil, you motherfucker, you can't have any part of me because I'm a child of God! Almighty God, Jesus Christ, the angels and me, beat your evil ass. We'll continue to beat you. You have been rebuked!"

Michelle almost choked on her gum. She wasn't used to hearing her mother use that kind of language and I seldom do, but when I'm mad the words will fall out of my mouth and I have no control. I was furious because the devil planted cancer in my body and I'd been through mortal hell with chemo and the horrible side effects.

"Well, what a paradox. You're cussing the devil and praising God with the same breath," Michelle said, with a snicker.

"I know, but God knows my heart. It's only words and God has heard much worse from people who have evil hearts. My heart is full of love."

Facebook post: December 11th, 2018. I know most people have heard of survivor remorse. I think I feel a similar thing with my cancer being in total remission. So many of my wonderful friends are battling the same beast and have been for a long time, yet they haven't reached remission, and here I am rejoicing from my wonderful news. How I wish I could wave a magic wand and cure all of my precious friends and others that I don't even know. My prayers are with all. Prayers do work. I'm living proof. God bless each and every one.

Note from my journal: I've finally lost my ever-lovin' mind. I was watching a Christmas movie on Lifetime. It was the first Christmas a mother's daughter had come home for in three years. The mother criticized and contradicted everything her daughter said and did. I yelled at the TV, "And you wonder why it took her three years to come back home!" Then I told the daughter to pack up and leave. I think I need to turn off the TV and play with Olivia.

That night, Olivia tucked me in bed as she does every night. And the blankets had to be under my chin. "I love you, Nana."

"I love you too, sweetie. May I have a kiss?"

"No. You have to wait until December 25th." Out the door she went.

I kept waiting for Olivia to mention my loss of hair, but at that point she hadn't seemed to notice. However, a couple days later, she said, "Nana, your hair is different."

"Yes, honey, it is. The medicine I take makes my hair fall out."

"You're sure gonna be ugly when you get bald."

In a sarcastic tone I said, "Well, thanks a lot!"

"You're very welcome." Out the door she went.

I didn't take chemo anymore but I had to go to the cancer center so they could flush my port, do blood work and take vitals. They also ran bags of stuff that I wasn't sure what it was through me to flush out the toxins. Michelle and I were on time, but the lady at the desk where I register and get my wristband wasn't there.

What we didn't know was nine people had shown up at the same time right before I got there. After a thirty minute wait, I was registered and my wristband was put on me. I waited another twenty minutes before I was called back. A nurse took me to the prep room where I was asked the same eighty questions five times. Another nurse flushed my port and she didn't have any trouble getting the blood.

It was time to take me to my room for my infusion. No rooms were available. I had to wait another twenty minutes for a room. Finally, I got to a room and a nurse brought in the last machine they have left to hook up my bags. The machine didn't work for more than thirty minutes at a time. It just shut down. The beeper would go off for twenty minutes before anybody could get to me.

Four times the machine stopped working. What should have been no more than an hour and a half turned out to be three hours. Finally, my bags were empty, it was time to flush my port with Heparin, and I'd be ready to go. No order or code number was in the computer for me and the nurse couldn't unlock the cabinet. I waited another twenty minutes for them to get it straightened out. Finally, I was flushed, needle was out of my port and I was ready to go. I couldn't wait to get out of there. I reached the front door, walked outside and it was pouring rain. All ten of the hairs I have left on my head were soaked.

We made it to the car and I dried my hairs on a towel that Michelle had in the back seat. "I'm ready for an ice cream cone."

"Me, too. We'll stop at the Big Dipper and get one. Ice cream makes everything better."

I can't remember when ice cream had tasted that good. It relieved my stress and I felt like a child. "It's the little things, honey. Who would have ever thought an ice cream cone could do wonders for my stressful day. I'm feeling good now. Let's get on home so I can play with Olivia.

"You feel good because you're jacked up on Decadron."

"Good. When we get home I'm going to go up and down the ten basement steps at least ten times."

Michelle gave me the 'look'. I just laughed. I knew I couldn't do ten times, but I was going to try for five. I also knew in a couple days, I'd bottom out. Coming down from a steroid wasn't a good feeling.

Chapter Twenty-Two

December was rolling on by. I was getting stronger by the day. By the 19th, I was making trips up and down the basement steps eight times a day. I pushed hard and sometimes I had to stop midway and take a breather, then climb on. I was determined to up my trips to twelve a day before Christmas.

Note from my journal: December 19th, 2018. Parents and grandparents were invited to the school Christmas party today. I wanted so badly to go and be with Olivia, but I wasn't strong enough. I admit my eyes leaked, but God willing I'll be there next year. My hair is still falling out. I tried to do a comb over to hide my bald spots and ended up looking like Donald Trump. Heaven forbid.

Olivia came home all excited. She ran into my room and told me about her great day at the Christmas party. She had a bag full of presents, and she pulled them out one by one and told me who they were from. I was as excited as she was.

After supper, Olivia and I played school. She was the teacher. I had to read seven books by Dr. Seuss. After I read them aloud I had to write down four words from a page she called out. I did. She looked at my paper and said, "You didn't write on the third line. You need to pay attention and follow instructions!" She gave me an F. I was glad I wasn't on TV or I would have had to look in the camera and say, "I'm not smarter than a kindergartner."

I had no adequate words to describe the joy that Olivia brought me. I knew the happiness she brought to my life was the medicine that I needed to make me stronger.

As time went on, I learned that sometimes it pays to just sit back and listen. I would laugh when I overheard conversations with Olivia and Michelle. I was writing in my journal when I heard the two of them going at each other.

"Olivia Anne Eakins, please stop singing so I can hear the news! Don't make me put you on the naughty list."

"Mama Anne Eakins, you just ruined a perfectly good Christmas. You're the naughty one!"

I put down my journal and laughed. I knew the conversation wasn't over. Then I heard her footsteps running. Olivia ran into my bedroom.

"Hi, sweetie."

"Nana, can I stay in here with you?"

"Sure, honey. Why would you even ask? You know you can come to Nana, anytime. What's got you upset?"

"Mommy is driving me nuts!"

"I think it's the other way around. You've been a pistol today. But you keep my heart happy.

"I'm glad I make you happy, Nana. I love you. You're the best nana in the whole world."

My heart melted. She had worn her mother out, and I was the only one who was going to put up with her shenanigans.

December 20th, 2018, I got the phone call I had been anxiously waiting for. Doctor S's office called. I had an appointment to see him the next day. I never thought I'd ever be happy to have surgery, but at that time I could barely contain myself. I wanted it done and over with. Then I knew my new life would begin.

It was hard for me to go to sleep that night. So many things kept running through my mind. I pictured all the things that Olivia and I would do come spring. I'd be healthy and strong and we'd play outside, dig in the dirt, plant flowers, make mud pies and I'd live the childhood with her that I had been robbed of. I prayed with all my heart, and fell asleep before I said, "Amen."

The next morning, Olivia came into my bedroom. "Nana, it's time to wake up. Mommy is fixing your breakfast."

"Okay, sweetie. Are you going to eat breakfast with me?"

"Nah, I done ate."

"What did you eat?"

"I ate crackers and drank milk."

"That's all you ever eat. I've got to work with you and get you to eat different things. You can't live on crackers and milk for the rest of your life."

"I don't want to hear you," she said, and ran off to her play room.

I slipped on my robe and went into the kitchen. Michelle had fixed me scrambled eggs with bacon and toast. My taste buds were back to normal, and I enjoyed every bite. Keeping my word to Doctor A, I ate every two hours. And I had worked up to ten trips up and down he basement steps. I felt strong and I no longer required a nap in the afternoons. I was almost back to being my normal self. It had been a long seven months.

My appointment was for 2 p.m. I was antsy for the rest of the morning, but I passed the time by playing with Olivia, and making trips up and down the basement steps. I seemed to have more bounce in my steps.

We made the trip to Evansville, and I hoped that Doctor S was as good as Doctor A said he was. However, I had already turned it over to God, and I knew He would pull me through.

I was calm and collected when my name was called. We went into an exam room, and a nurse started with the questions. I have no idea why all the questions irritated me. All my answers were in the computer. Doctor M and Doctor A had sent the images of all my scans, my treatments, and all the information they needed. However, I realize it's necessary and I was being nitpicky. I've always been a cut-to-the chase person, so to speak, so I made up my mind to stop letting the little but necessary things get to me.

Doctor S came into the exam room, introduced himself, shook hands, and he did cut to the chase to the point he didn't give me time to ask a few questions. "I'll do my best to do your surgery robotic, which means you'll have five small incisions. If I can't do it robotic, then I'll make a midline incision from your belly button to your pubic bone. I'm going to take out your ovaries, fallopian tubes and while I'm in there I'll take out your appendix. I'll also scrape your colon and do a rapid test to see if there are any cancer cells in the colon. If so, then I'll try to take out part of your intestines and fuse them back together—"

When he made that statement, my mind couldn't accept the possibility of cancer being in my colon. My brain traveled to another dimension. I didn't hear the rest of what he said. I came back to reality when he said he was going to do a pelvic exam. "Undress from the waist down and I'll be back in few minutes."

I felt as if I were a robot being controlled by another person as I undressed. The nurse put my feet in stirrups, and again my mind traveled off. I snapped back to reality quickly when Doctor S examined me. The pain was unbearable and I screamed. I did my best to hold back, but I couldn't.

When he was finished with the pelvic exam he said, "I don't feel anything on your ovaries. The tumors have shrunk. That's good. Get dressed and the nurse will explain anything you're not sure about." He headed to the door.

I knew I had to find my humor, as warped as it is at times, because it was the only thing that was going to hold me together. I said, "Doctor A, I'm bald. After you take out what I can live without, would you do a hair transplant?"

He laughed and said, "I would if I could, but that's not my field."

I saw the look of relief on Michelle's face. Her silly mother was back.

I dressed and sat in a chair. The nurse asked me if I had any questions. "No. I understand everything. All I want to hear is the date for my surgery."

"The office will call you when we get you on his schedule."

"I hope it's soon," I said. "I want this rotten cancer out of me."

"I understand," she said. "Someone will give you a call in a few days."

We left the office and I shut my mind off. I enjoyed the Christmas decorations that were everywhere I looked. The streets were lined with beautiful lights, wreaths and ribbons around poles. Small Christmas trees were decorated in the medians along the sidewalks. Large Christmas trees were decorated in the windows of restaurants and stores. The trip home was made in silence. I didn't want to talk. I just wanted to enjoy the beauty.

When we got home, Olivia was waiting at the front door. When I walked inside, she hugged me and said, "Where did you go? I thought you left me again."

"Nana had to go to the doctor. I'm not going to leave you, honey. Do you want me to tell you about the surgery I'm going to have done?"

"What's surgery?"

"Let's go to my bedroom and I'll explain it. I've got pictures that will help you understand it."

Before I had left the doctor's office I was handed a packet with all the instructions that I had to do before and after surgery. The packet contained a picture of a woman's abdominal organs. We sat side by side in the recliner. I showed her the picture and told her what each organ was and what Doctor S was going to take out.

"How is he gonna get them out?" she asked.

"He's going to make a few incisions in Nana's belly. Incisions are little cuts. He'll reach inside the cuts and take everything out." I pulled up my sweater and pulled down the top of my pants. "This is where he's going to cut me." I pointed to five spots.

"Is it gonna hurt?"

"No, Nana won't feel a thing. Another doctor will give me some medicine and it'll make me go sound asleep and it'll numb me. I'll just take a long nap. When I wake up, the surgery will be over."

She held the picture and studied it for a few minutes. She pointed to all the organs and called out the names. She's a child that only needs to be told something once and she remembers. She seemed to be okay with my explanation. I was glad I had the pictures to show her.

I was up early Christmas morning. I was still like a child and I couldn't wait to watch everybody open presents, and I was anxious to open my presents, too. We all gathered in the living room and Julia played Santa and handed out presents. Olivia grabbed a present and ran to me.

"Nana, you open your present from me first."

I ripped off the paper and pulled out a small box. Olivia's eyes were saying, *open it.*

I pulled out a figurine. It was a teddy bear holding a sign that read, 'World's Greatest Grandma'. I held back my tears. "This is the sweetest and best Christmas present that I've ever gotten. I'll keep it forever."

"I'm glad you like it. I bought it at the Christmas bazaar at my school. I paid two dollars for it."

"Well, this two-dollar present is worth a million dollars to Nana."

"Okay," she said as she whirled around. "Which ones are my presents? I've waited long enough."

Julia said, "You can read. Look at the tags."

She shuffled through the stacks of presents and pulled out each one with her name on it. I watched her rip off paper, and her eyes brightened as she held up each present. In my mind's eye I could see my three babies opening their presents on Christmas morning. It was as if I were in a time warp.

I was determined to pull a prank on somebody for Christmas, but everybody was on to me and it's hard to do, but I did it. I always give my granddaughter, Julia, money because what do you buy a teenager that pleases them. She opened her Christmas card and pulled out a one-dollar bill. She smiled, waved the bill in the air and said, "Thank you Nana."

I tried to convince her that I thought I had put a one hundred-dollar bill in the card, but she didn't buy it.

"I'm on to you, Nana. You can't fool me like you used to when I was little."

My prank was a bust, but we all laughed and that was good enough. Later I gave her the amount of money I had put back for her.

After the presents had been opened, I helped Michelle cook a big breakfast. I was hungry, and since my taste buds were back to life it was delicious. After we had eaten, we rinsed off our plates and stacked them in the dishwasher. Then Michelle, Julia, Olivia, and I gathered in my bedroom. Olivia brought in all her Christmas presents and we played with her. She had gotten tons of things to play with, but her favorite was her cymbals I had gotten her. She ran through the house banging them until we had a headache. She's always loved any kind of musical instrument.

Michelle, Julia, and I spent the afternoon reminiscing Christmases past and the pranks I played on the family and a few they managed to play on me. Later in the evening we gathered around the kitchen table and ate a pecan cheese ball with dill pickles, a tradition we had been doing since all my children were still home.

Cathye had Christmas with her two daughters and six grandchildren. They all called and wished me a Merry Christmas and they told me they loved me. My heart overflowed with joy. It had been a wonderful Christmas.

I took time to make my ten trips up and down the basement steps. By ten o'clock I was tired. I was getting ready to get into the shower and call it a day. Just as I headed toward the bathroom my cell phone rang. I didn't recognize the number but I answered it.

My heart skipped a beat when I heard my son's voice. "Mom, a guard was kind enough to let me use his personal cell phone. I only have a minute. Merry Christmas. I love you."

"I love you too, son. Merry Christmas to you. I'm so glad you called, you topped off my day."

"How are you doing?"

"I'm doing great. I'm—" Click. I supposed the guard had taken his phone back before he got caught.

Lending an inmate a personal cell phone was against the rules. I "God blessed" whoever he was for being kind-hearted and letting my son call me. His sweet voice made my mother's heart cry with joy. How I longed to see him and hug him.

I took a shower and I could still hear his voice in my head though the banging of cymbals made it hard. By the time I was ready for bed, Michelle had taken the cymbals and hidden them. Olivia came into my room so she could tuck me in as she did every night. I asked, "This is December the twenty-fifth. Do I get the kiss you promised me?"

"You sure do." She kissed my check. I kissed her forehead and she tucked me in, turned out the bed-side table lamp and said, "Goodnight. I love you and Merry Christmas."

"I love you, my little darling, and thank you for my present. It was the best one I got."

She giggled and went out of the room. She always shut my door. I lay in bed and listened to her footsteps running down the short hallway to her bed-room. Tears ran as I thanked God for a wonderful day. I loved being with my girls, and it was wonderful hearing from my oldest daughter, her daughters and my great-grandchildren. Scott's three children didn't call me, and my heart longed to hear from them, but getting to hear from my son was the greatest gift I could have gotten. I fell asleep as his voice still echoed in my head.

I woke up an hour later when I heard the clang of cymbals. Olivia had found them and she was going to bang them one more time before her mother hid them again. I decided I'd post something on Facebook. I was going to start out sincere and end it with a joke. So many friends have told me that on bad days, they look forward to my post because I always make them smile. I liked the feeling of knowing I had brought a little happiness to somebody.

Facebook post: December 25th, 2018. I don't like to wish time away as it goes too fast, but I'll be glad to say goodbye to 2018. It's been a pisser of a year, starting with last Jan 5th, and it has continued to get worse. But I've maintained my sense of humor and laughed through the tears and the pain. I will continue to look for the bright side of every situation even when my world is dark. God has brought me a long way and I know that He will guide me through what lies ahead as long as I keep the faith and my spirit keeps fighting for brighter days. Thank you my wonderful Facebook friends for your prayers and well wishes. They have given me strength and determination. I *will* kick cancer's ass! I've had a great Christmas. My daughter cooked a great meal and she let me have a bite of everything. I hid food under my bed in case she puts me back on Kibbles and Bits tomorrow.

Chapter Twenty-Three

Note from my journal: December 26th, 2018. I got the call from Doctor S's office. My surgery is scheduled for January 9th, 2019. I'm like a prisoner with a calendar on my cell wall, marking off days until my surgery. I'll be so glad when it's over. Per orders of General Michelle, I'm not allowed to post on Facebook until I'm off all pain meds. Nobody will know the difference, because I'm always silly. Being under the influence will sound normal to my friends in Facebook Land.

The week after Christmas rolled on by, I was still making trips up and down the basement steps and I was feeling strong. I didn't need any assistance with whatever I needed to do. Keeping with tradition for New Year's Day, my daughter cooked black-eyed peas, cabbage, corn beef and cornbread, which according to the older people was supposed to bring good luck for the coming year. It was one of my favorite meals. It smelled so good and my taste buds were ready. I fixed a plate, sat down at the kitchen table and took a big bite of peas. Suddenly, I felt like a cartoon character. Tears filled my eyes, I knew that flames were shooting from my nostrils and smoke was coming out of my ears. She had put jalapeno peppers in them.

"Good lord, Michelle! I'm on fire! Now my year is ruined! Just ruined! From now on I really will eat Kibbles and Bits."

"I can barely taste the jalapeno peppers, but I forgot you can't eat anything spicy. I'm sorry. The cabbage, corn beef and cornbread aren't hot, and we both know that eating black-eyed peas for good luck is just a myth. You ate them last year and you see how the year turned out. Good grief!"

"I just got my taste buds back and you refried them!" I was chugging water and finally the fire in my mouth went out. The rest of the meal was good.

I saw her snicker. I laughed too.

Facebook post: January 2nd, 2019. It's been one month and three days since I've had a chemo infusion. I just counted the hairs on my head. I've gone from ten to twelve. I bet I have at least fifteen in another month. Surgery is one week from today. I'll be so glad when it's over. By spring I'll come alive just like the world after a long winter's nap.

Note from my journal: January 3rd, 2019. I just talked with my surgical nurse. She asked at least fifty questions and gave me at least fifty instructions for me to do and not do before surgery. She was sweet and she put me at ease when I asked her a few questions. She said there was a possibility that I would stay in the hospital for three days, and she told me what I couldn't do after surgery.

I said, "Well, I guess a bottle of Jack Daniel's and a pack of smokes are just totally out of the question, eh?"

She laughed and said, "If it were allowed I'd join you with both."

Michelle was fighting ants, which I call piss-ants, with everything on the market. The kitchen counter tops, the bathroom counter tops and the bedside table in my room were covered. Olivia and I were doing hand to hand combat and mashing them with our thumbs. Olivia thought it was a fun game, but I wasn't too thrilled.

I was sitting in the recliner and Olivia said, "Nana, can I sit on your bed and eat my crackers and drink my milk?"

"Sure, honey. You can climb into Nana's bed, but pull off your dirty socks."

She pulled off her socks and got comfortable while she watched cartoons. I was about to OD on cartoons, but whatever made her happy, made me happy. When she finished eating, she jumped off the bed and scampered off. The recliner was uncomfortable for me, so I decided I'd take advantage of my bed while Olivia was occupied with something else.

I pulled back the top sheet and found out Olivia had dropped cracker crumbs all over my bed. I swiped them off and climbed in, hoping no ants had had time to find them. I watched a movie and since no ants were crawling on me I figured I was safe.

The next morning I found my laptop covered with cracker crumbs, and a hundred piss- ants were have a feast. I mashed as many ants as I could with my fist and wiped off the cracker crumbs. When I raised the top I saw ants crawling across the key-board. I started hitting keys and smashing the little pests. I knew it wouldn't be long before the keys would stick from all the dead ant bodies.

Note from my journal: January 4th, 2019. This is always a hard day for me to get through because it is the date that my mother and little brother were killed. The three of us were struck by a speeding car. The angels saved me that night for reasons, some of which I've figured out, and some I haven't. It doesn't matter. I'm alive. Sixty-eight years later on this date I start my prep for surgery. I have to do a five-day prep. Once again the angels are going to save me. Cancer will be gone and it will never return. This I believe with all my soul.

Note from my journal: January 5th, 2019. It's a cool, crisp day, but the sun is shining and I sat out-side. The only time I stick my head out the door is when I go to the doctor or hospital. It was so wonderful to be able to go outdoors and enjoy the sunshine. It's the little things that I used to take for granted that now bring me much pleasure.

January 7th, 2019, I had to drink a sixteen ounce bottle of Miralax at 4 p.m. I knew it was going to taste horrible and I dreaded it. Michelle had put it in the fridge, hoping if it was cold I would be able to get it down easier. She brought me the bottle. I unscrewed the cap. I took a sip. Much to my surprise and delight, it had virtually no taste. I chugged it down. "Not bad," I said, as I handed Michelle the empty bottle. "When it starts to work, everybody better clear the room. I just hope I can make it to the potty chair in time."

"Don't worry about it. I changed you and cleaned you before. I can do it this time."

By 6 p.m., the Miralax began its job. I made it to the potty chair every time. By 10 p.m., I told Michelle to go to bed. We had to be at the hospital by 6:30 a.m. Olivia tucked me in and she and Michelle kissed me goodnight.

I was on the potty chair every ten minutes until 4:30 a.m. the next morning. I had no idea that much crap could come out of a person my size.

Michelle opened my bedroom door at 5 a.m. "You're already up? I'll get the Gatorade. You have to get 32 ounces down by five-thirty, then nothing until after surgery."

"I've been awake all night. The last time I crapped was thirty minutes ago. I sure hope I'm done. I think my guts and brains are in the potty chair. You might want to rinse them off. I'll need them." I laughed, trying to keep my sense of humor because I knew if I lost my humor, then I'd lose control of my emotions which were threatening tears. "I tried to empty it every time I used it, but there were a few times when I couldn't. It stinks in here and it's making me sick."

Michelle glanced over at the potty chair. "I don't see any guts or brains and if they are in there I'm not going to fish them out and rinse them off. I'll empty it though. It smells like something crawled up your butt and died."

We laughed, though we both knew we were putting on a brave front. She brought me the bottle of Gatorade and I chugged it.

Michelle came back into my room at 5:45 a.m. "Are you ready?"

"All I have to do is pee, slip on my robe and house slippers. They'll strip me as soon as I get there. I see no point in putting on clothes. I sure hope I don't crap myself on the way."

"Me, too. I'll have to roll down the windows and it's cold out there."

Joy Redmond

We were at the hospital and I was in the surgical prep room by 6:30. I was nervous but anxious to get it over with.

Chapter Twenty-Four

The surgical prep nurse was kind and efficient. She took me to a private room, helped me undress and put on what looked like a zip-up blue bag instead of the usual hospital gown. I noticed there was a hole on the right side with a cap over it. "What is the hole for?"

"It's there in case you get cold. I can put a tube in the hole and blow hot air into the gown. It'll keep you toasty."

"That's good to know. I freeze all the time." I was amazed.

We went back to the prep room. Michelle was sitting in a chair close by. "I love the outfit. But you really need shoes and a bag to match," she said. We laughed.

Nurse P told me she had to start two IV's. I told her I didn't have a working vein, but I had a port. She informed me that she couldn't use the port because the anesthetic would go straight to my heart.

I said, "Well, good luck in finding veins. People on the IV trauma team can't find one." My nerves were getting the best of me. I knew she wasn't going to find one working vein let alone two.

"Just relax and let me do my job. I'm better than the IV trauma team. And if by chance I can't find two, then the anesthesiologist will find one. He's trained better than anybody. He can find one in your neck if all else fails."

I closed my eyes and prayed that she'd be able to find veins that wouldn't blow.

She inserted the needle between my little finger and ring finger on my left hand. It worked. I sighed with relief. She did the same with my right hand.

"Good job," I said. "But watch them closely because they might blow at any minute."

"I've got my eye on you. I'll know before you do if they are going to blow. I need to ask a few questions, then I'll explain the procedure."

I wondered how many times the procedure would be explained to me. I understood it the first time. However, I knew she was doing her job and I knew there were people who didn't always understand.

"Doctor S is going to scrape your colon and do a rapid test to see if the cancer is in your colon. If so, then he will try to remove several feet of your intestines and fuse them back. If he can't do that, then he'll make three incisions and attach a colostomy bag. He—"

My mind clearly comprehended and I didn't let her finish. I screamed, "No! No! No! I don't want to hear it."

"You have to hear it. You have to accept that it might have to be done," she firmly stated. "Once you're healed it can be reversed. You won't have a colostomy bag for the rest of your life."

I broke down and cried louder than a newborn. I couldn't and wouldn't accept it. Then I went into hard shakes. My entire body shook and trembled as if I were having a seizure. Nurse P inserted a tube into the hole of my gown, and the hot air stopped the shakes. I knew I had to pull myself together, but I couldn't. I continued to cry.

Michelle said, "Mom, Doctor S explained this to you the day we went for your consultation with him. Why are you acting like this? It won't be permanent."

I knew Michelle was put out with me and it pissed me off. "You're not the one who'll be wearing a bag of shit on your side. I will. I'm the one who'll be going through this. Not you!" I didn't tell her that my mind had traveled off when Doctor S had mentioned it. She had no idea that I didn't know everything that had been explained to me.

"You're right. I'm sorry. I just thought you—"

Before Michelle finished her sentence, my oldest daughter, Cathye and her two daughters, Christina and Crystal came into the room and I broke down again.

Nurse P said, "She can't go into surgery in her state of mind."

Cathye took my hand. "What's wrong, Mom? I thought you were anxious to get this done and over with."

I was crying so hard I couldn't talk. Nurse P explained what might have to be done. I saw Cathye throw her hands over her face and I saw tears well. I cried harder.

Nurse P came to my side and said, "Open your mouth."

I opened my mouth and she put two small pills on my tongue, then she held a small cup of water to my lips. "Swallow."

There was no more than five drops of water in the cup, but I swallowed the pills. At that point I would have chewed them if the water hadn't washed them down. Cathye held my hand and said, "Mom, if this is what it takes to save your life, it has to be done. You said you wanted to live. Right?"

I said, "Yes, I want to live. I'll do whatever it takes to save me."

My granddaughters were in shock and they didn't know what to say. They shed tears as their mother talked to me.

A few minutes later another nurse came into the room. She introduced herself and said she was going to make three spots on my abdomen where the colostomy bag would be placed.

I thought I had myself under control because the pills had me a bit loopy, but when she mentioned a colostomy bag I broke down. I was ready to jump off the table, grab my clothes and cancel the surgery.

Both daughters stood by my side as Nurse P unzipped the gown. I think they had read my thoughts and they were ready to grab me in case I tried to bolt from the room. She marked three spots, but I closed my eyes and refused to look. I wasn't going to accept that it was even a remote possibility. It wasn't going to happen. My mind shut off.

A few minutes later the anesthesiologist came into the room. He introduced himself, then he went into the same speech about my colon and a colostomy bag.

I yelled, "I've heard it. I don't want to hear anymore!"

Michelle said, "The more you talk about it, the more she's going to get upset."

He said, "Okay. I'll be back to get her in a few minutes."

Before he left I said, "Nurse P found two veins but my veins blow easily. I don't want them to blow and wake me up during surgery."

"I'll watch you closely. I know when veins are going to blow. Should it happen, and it's doubtful, I'll have Doctor Q in the OR, and he'll have an IV in your neck before you have a chance to wake up. You're in good hands."

"I'm in God's hands," I said. At that moment I felt warm hands wrap around my body. Peace flowed through me. I knew God was holding me, and I knew the angels were wrapping their loving wings around me.

Soon, the anesthesiologist and a surgical nurse came to get me. The nurse slipped a surgical cap over my head. I was calm and my sense of humor came to my rescue. I said, "There you go messing up my beautiful hair. All five strands."

She laughed and said, "I've got a bad habit of doing that." She patted my arm. "I'll be with you through the surgery. I'll keep a close eye on you. I've been working in the OR for thirty years."

"That's good to know," I said. "You have experience. I don't like the young whippersnappers who think they know it all and they don't know shit." The pills had hit me hard and my potty mouth was in full force. I'm surprised I didn't call somebody a sonofabitch. The nurse was walking fast trying to keep up as I was being pushed down long halls and turning corners. I could actually feel a breeze around me as I was whisked into the OR.

I looked around the room and saw several people. I knew they were the surgical team and I prayed they would be on their toes. I looked over my head and said, "Hey, Mr. Sandman, before you put the mask over my face I want to say something."

"Say whatever you want."

I yelled and I do mean yelled, "Cancer, kiss my ass!" I heard several people laugh.

The mask was placed over my face and I knew I only had a few seconds. I mumbled, "Bring me back, God. Please bring me bac...."

The next thing I knew, I was in my hospital room. I looked around and though everybody was a blur, I knew my family was surrounding me. I managed to mumble, "Aw, my babies are here."

I faded into darkness.

Chapter Twenty-Five

My children told me that I was in recovery for two hours because they had a hard time getting me to come around. I vaguely remember looking around my hospital room and seeing my family.

My granddaughter, Crystal, fed me ice chips. She was spooning ice chips into my mouth as fast as she could and she could barely keep up with me as I opened my mouth for more.

My granddaughter, Christina, made sure that I had warm blankets over me at all times. As soon as the ones that were over me started to cool, she told a nurse to bring more warm ones.

Cathye said, "Mom, there's an ice pack on your stomach. If you feel something it isn't a colostomy bag, so don't freak out."

"You've already told me."

"I didn't tell you."

"Well, Michelle told me."

Michelle said, "I didn't tell you."

A nurse was covering me with warm blankets and she said, "The nurse in recovery probably told you."

In my mind I could vividly hear a female voice saying, "You don't have a colostomy bag. Doctor S didn't remove any part of your colon. He took out your ovaries, fallopian tubes and appendix."

I vividly remembered saying, "Thank God." To this day I'm assuming the recovery nurse did tell me. That's all the memory I have of being in recovery. I later learned the anesthesiologist had over-juiced me. I don't remember being in any pain. I'm sure I was, but if I couldn't remember it, then as far as I was concerned, I wasn't.

Michelle told me that I said I was hurting when I was brought from recovery to my room, and the nurse told me she couldn't give me anything for pain because I wasn't out from under the anesthetic well enough. I don't recall being in any pain the whole time I was there, and I thank God.

That night my sister, Linda and my niece, Debbie, came to see me. Debbie said, "I hear your doctor is a cutie."

"Yeah, but he's an asshole," I said. My subconscious was remembering Doctor W, and he *was* an asshole. Doctor S was kind and I liked him.

Linda said, "You have a wonderful nurse taking care of you."

"Yeah, but she's an asshole," I said. "Is Nameless here?"

"Yes, he's over there in a chair. Do you see him?" Cathye said.

"Nah. I can't see who anybody is. But he's a good man." I'm glad I didn't say he was an asshole since I thought everybody else was.

I went to sleep and the next thing I remember was looking out the window and it was dark. I looked around the room. Everybody was gone except Michelle. When I opened my eyes, she came to my side. "Mom, we've been trying to wake you up all day. Can you stay awake for a little while and talk to me?"

"I'll try. My eyes don't want to stay open and my throat feels like it's paralyzed. It's hard to swallow."

"I know. The nurses managed to rouse you enough to get pain pills down you, but you gagged and they came back up three times before you could swallow them."

"I don't remember that. I don't understand why I'm having a hard time swallowing. Maybe my throat is messed up from being intubated during surgery."

"That's what the nurse said, but you were over-juiced with anesthetic. I'm not going to leave you."

"Honey, I'll be fine. The nurses will take care of me. You can't sleep sitting up in a chair, and that bench thing isn't long enough for you to stretch out. Please go home. Get some rest. I know you're worn out."

"Well, since you're coming around and making sense I might go on. You've mumbled off and on all day, but nobody knew what you were trying to say. I'm scared."

"Don't be scared, honey. I'm in good hands. Please go home. And be careful. It's dark and I know you have a hard time driving at night."

"I'll be fine. Don't worry about me. I'll be back tomorrow as soon as I can." She kissed me goodbye, and I was asleep by the time she put her coat on and left the room.

A nurse woke me up. "I'm going to give you a shot in your stomach. It's a blood thinner. I'll show you how to do it because you have to give yourself an injection every night for the next two weeks."

I watched her pinch a half inch of skin, hold the pinch and insert the needle straight into my stomach. "Be sure you don't angle the needle. It has to be straight going in and coming out. Don't turn loose of the skin you pinch up until the syringe is empty. Make sure you pinch up the skin two inches from your belly button, and alternate right and left sides each night. After you empty the syringe and take the needle out, push the plunger again. It will automatically drop the needle in the syringe. Put the empty syringe into a large plastic bottle. Do you understand?"

"I understand. I can do it. No problem. I'm good with needles. I gave shots to people for thirty years before I retired."

"Great. Some people are terrified of needles and they can't do it. Remember to do it at the same time each night. It's ten o'clock, so you inject yourself at ten every night. It doesn't have to be right on the dot, but as close as possible."

"Needles are the least of my worries." I laughed and said, "I also know how to tell time."

Nurse laughed. "Then you'll be fine."

The next morning, a nurse got me out of bed and took me for a walk. There was a circle where they walked patients. I managed to make the circle, but my legs were trembling, and she supported my weight. She mostly carried me instead of me walking. I wanted to go back to bed but she said I had to sit in a chair.

I sat down in the chair beside my bed and I was exhausted. She told me I needed to eat breakfast. The last thing I wanted was food, but I knew I had to eat. "I'll try to eat a bowl of Rice Krispies," I said.

"I can get that for you. You don't have to order from the cafeteria. We keep a lot of food up here on the ward."

She brought me a small box of Rice Krispies, a bowl and a small carton of milk. I did my best to open the box and pour the cereal into the bowl. My coordination was off and it was a chore. I fumbled trying to open the carton of milk. Just as I was about to give up, a nurse came in and opened it for me. She poured the milk over the cereal and handed me a plastic spoon. "Eat up," she said, and left the room.

I dipped the spoon into the bowl and I thought I was headed for my mouth, but I hit the side of my face. I tried three more times but I couldn't hit the target. I placed the spoon on the tray, picked up the bowl and drank the cereal and milk. I placed the bowl on the tray and wiped my mouth. I was startled when Doctor S walked into the room.

"Good morning. Your color is good and I see you ate breakfast, and the nurse said that you made a lap around the circle," he said.

"Well, it's more like she carried me, but together we made it. I'm having a hard time swallowing—"

He cut me off and said, "You're going to be fine. I'll see you later."

Just like that he was out of the room. I had questions but he didn't give me a chance to ask them or a chance to tell him I was having difficulties. It pissed me off. Later, I told my nurse how brisk he was. She said, "He's that way. He's a great surgeon, but he doesn't take much time with patients. However, he's a busy man. He saw you sitting up and eating and that was all he needed. Plus he read what all the nurses had charted on the computer."

"I know this is modern day medicine but I don't like being treated as if I'm no more than notes in a computer. He didn't even look at my monitor. All my vitals are low."

The nurse didn't respond to my comment. She left the room.

I was tired of sitting up, and I managed to get out of the chair and back into the bed. It took all my strength, but it felt good to lay flat. Just as I closed my eyes, Michelle came into my room.

"Hi Mom. How do you feel today?"

"I'm not in any pain but I still can't swallow correctly. I keep watching my monitor and my vitals are off kilter. However, nobody seems to be worried about it. Doctor S came in but he didn't give me a chance to ask him anything or tell him anything."

"Well, I got a lot of questions to ask the nurse. And I will get answers! They're not going to ignore you while I'm here. You can bet on that!"

A nurse came into the room holding a pill cup. "It's time to take your pain pill."

"I'm not hurting. Why do you keep poking pills in me?"

"I'm going to make sure you stay pain free."

I put a capsule into my mouth and I couldn't get it down. I gagged and it came back up three times. The nurse kept pushing it back into my mouth and she held a glass of water, saying, "Swallow!"

"She's trying to swallow! She can't. There's something wrong," Michelle said. "Are you paying attention to her vitals? Her blood pressure is excessively low, her heart rate is rapid and her oxygen level has gone down. And unless you've recently emptied her catheter bag, she isn't putting out more than a tablespoon of urine every two hours. I checked her catheter bag all day yesterday and that's all she was doing then and there is a bag of fluids running through her. My mom pees every twenty minutes without fluids. That tells me her kidneys aren't properly working. You're a nurse and I know you know that I'm right."

The nurse dropped her head but she didn't say anything, which told me, she did know. However, I knew she wasn't allowed to give her opinion.

"I've charted everything in the computer. Doctor S has read my notes." She left the room. Twenty minutes later she came back and said that Doctor S was dismissing me.

Michelle seldom raises her voice, but at this point she was yelling. "Is he crazy? She's in no condition to go home. Evidently, he didn't read your notes. You get him on the phone and I'll talk to him."

"I'm not allowed to call him. I have to go through his nurse."

"Then you get his nurse on the phone. I'll talk to her."

"That isn't allowed. Only nurses talk with other nurses."

"So, his nurse is saying she can be dismissed?"

"Yes. My hands are tied. I do what the doctors and their nurses tell me."

"Did his nurse read the notes you put in the computer?"

"I'm assuming she did."

"Well, assuming is not good enough for me. Will you please call her back and tell her what you noted. Maybe she'll pay attention if you tell her instead of relying on her to pull up the information and actually read it."

"I'll call her again. I'll explain everything," Nurse said.

A few minutes later the nurse came back into my room. "She said to dismiss her."

"Well, I tell you what. If you dismiss her, I'll take her straight to the ER. If the ER doctor doesn't have sense enough to realize she isn't in any condition to be dismissed, and if he doesn't re-admit her, then I'll go off and leave her here. What are they going to do—push her out in the parking lot?"

The nurse threw her hands into the air and left the room.

Michelle is a laid back person, she takes things in stride, but when she's backed into a corner, she puts on the gloves and she comes out punching and she doesn't stop until she gets a TKO. George Foreman would back away from her. I was proud of her. In my head I was saying, *Give them hell.* I didn't say anything out loud. I knew my baby girl was in control. But I wanted to say, "I pity the fool who wants to go up against her."

When the nurse left the room, I said, "Honey, she has to do what she's told. I know I'm not ready to go home, but—"

"But nothing. I'm not taking you home to die! I'm not finished with them yet."

A few minutes later the nurse came back into the room. I saw Michelle bristle. I knew the war was far from being over. I just lay back and waited for the fireworks.

Nurse said, "She isn't being dismissed. We'll keep her another night."

"Thank you," Michelle said.

I laughed and said, "You reminded me of Shirley Maclaine in the movie Terms of Endearment. As a matter of fact, you outdid her."

Michelle slightly chuckled. "Yes, I did, and I wasn't acting."

"Sit down and calm down, honey. I'm staying. We'll see what tomorrow brings.

Chapter Twenty-Six

After Michelle left I closed my eyes and tried to pray. For months, I'd prayed with all my heart and soul. I could always feel God. I knew He was listening. It brought me peace. While under the influence of Dilaudid, it was as if there was a great barrier between God and me. I didn't feel as if He could hear me. I couldn't feel Him. It was as if my prayers were bouncing off the wall and slapping me in the face.

I never realized this could happen when a person was under the influence of any substance. It was a horrible feeling. I finally understood what my son had tried to tell me for years, as he is addicted to opioids . I realized how he must feel, and why he can't make progress. He had told me many times that he feels as if he is hitting brick walls and God has turned his back on him. I understood what he meant. It became clear to me that addicts suffer from a disease and the devil is going to do all possible to keep addicts from God and make sure the disease never stops until it kills them. I learned a valuable lesson that night, though it was hard for me to accept that there was a distance between me and God.

The next morning I woke up when a nurse came into my room with a pill. I said, "I'm not going to take Dilaudid." I pushed it away.

"This is Ibuprofen. Six hundred milligrams. We've been alternating Tylenol and Ibuprofen every four hours through the night."

I had no memory of taking pills through the night. I accepted the pill and I was surprised and delighted that I got it down the first try. After I took the pill the nurse got me out of bed and walked me around the circle, twice. I was still a bit wobbly, but my balance was better than it was the day before. She told me I had to sit in the chair for one hour.

After my walk, I felt hungry, which I took as a good sign, and I ordered breakfast. I managed to hit my mouth and I ate two scrambled eggs, two pieces of bacon and a piece of toast. I swallowed with no difficulty.

I thought Doctor S would come by again, but he didn't.

I was tired of sitting in the chair, so I decided to take a walk around the circle by myself. I staggered and veered off course a few times but I made it. When I got back to my room, I got into bed. My legs were trembling, but I was proud of myself. I knew I had to push with all I had in order to gain strength. I couldn't give in to wanting to stay in bed and sleep.

Michelle didn't come until 2 p.m. I could tell she was ready to spar, but when I told her how I was doing, she gave a sigh of relief and her bristles lowered.

At 2:30 p.m., the nurse came in and told me I had been dismissed. Michelle looked at me, "What do you think?"

"I think I'm ready. I pitched a fit last night and the nurse took my catheter out. I'm going on my own and though I can't see the amount by the measuring lines, it looks like I'm doing plenty by just eyeballing it. That thing was painful and driving me crazy. My vitals are still off kilter a bit, but the nurse said I wasn't in any danger. I really want to go home and get in my comfortable bed."

"If you think you're ready, then I'll take you. You look and sound much better than you did yesterday. I'll help you dress, wait for the discharge papers, and we're out of here."

By the time I was dressed in my PJ's and robe, the nurse came back in, handed Michelle three prescriptions and a sample pack of syringes and needles. I explained about the shots I had to inject myself with.

"Can you do it, Mom?"

"Sure. I might need you to take the cap off the needle and pinch up my skin, but I won't have any problem injecting myself."

"I can pinch up your skin, but don't ask me to stick a needle in you."

"Mama has got this."

The nurse said, "She won't have any trouble. She seems confident. I need you to pull your car to the front of the hospital and I'll bring her out."

"Don't I get discharge papers?" I asked. No papers were necessary. Everything was done by computer. I asked if I had to wait for a wheelchair.

The nurse said, "No. I'll walk you out."

It felt as if I had walked ten miles before I reached the lobby. My legs were trembling and before I reached the entrance my knees buckled. The nurse steadied me and we continued. She opened the car door for me, assisted me inside, wished me well, then she was on her way.

"Things sure have changed in the medical profession," I said. "It seems like they take shortcuts with everything. And everything is electronic. Which I guess is faster, but in my opinion it isn't as efficient. But I'm old school. Just get me home, honey. The worst is behind me."

"Yes, it is. And you've done well." She chuckled and said, "Except for your meltdown in surgical prep. You've been a trouper through all the chemo and surgery. You're a strong woman with a fighting spirit. If I ever have to face what you've been through, God forbid, I hope I'm half as strong as you've been."

"I gave it to God, and He pulled me through. He always will. God gives me the strength to keep fighting and keep going. Doctor S took out my rotten ovaries, I'm cancer free."

"I sure hope so. You never thought this would happen to you and neither did I, yet here we are."

"I never in a million years thought that I'd have cancer. Cancer hit other people, not me. But as you said, here we are. You know sometimes we have to let go of the picture of what we thought life would be and learn to find the joy in the story that we're living. God has opened my eyes, my ears, and my mind to a lot since I was diagnosed. I take joy from it and I'm thankful."

"I need more of your kind of strength, courage, and faith."

"It comes with age. When the chips are down, we find faith, strength, and courage that we don't realize we have. And talk about strength. You've had more than most people. You've taken care of a five-year-old and took care of me when I was so sick I was like talking care of a newborn. Plus you took care of the house, shopping, laundry, and everything else that goes with running a house. I've worn you out, but you've never complained."

"You're my mother. I'll take care of you until I drop."

"I know, honey. And you know that your sister and brother would take care of me if not for the situation they're in at this time. It hurts them that they can't take me full-time, but Cathye helps as much as possible."

"I know they would. And I know it hurts them because they can't at this time. They feel like they are letting you down. And I'd worry myself silly if you were with anybody but me."

"You've been like a mother hen and I don't have enough words to express my gratefulness. So yes, you're as strong as I am, you don't give yourself enough credit."

"I suppose so. I hope I'm never put to the test as you've been." She fell silent for a few minutes as we drove down the main streets of Henderson. "I'm going to stop at the drugstore and drop off your prescriptions. I'll come back and pick them up after I get you home and settled in."

"I'll call Nameless. He'll pick them up and bring them to me. He's probably waiting to hear if I'm home. The twenty mile drive is nothing to him."

"I'm sure he and Aunt Linda will be out as soon as I call them. They were before surgery. They were a big help to me. They brought food and anything else you needed. They'll do the same now."

"Yes, they did. I'm sure they still will. I'm blessed to have them in my life."

We pulled into the driveway and I saw Olivia standing at the front window. She was waving her hand and I could read her lips, "Nana is home!"

Marcus hurried out to the car and assisted me into the house. Olivia opened the front door and threw her arms around my waist. "Nana, you came home! Can I see your surgery?"

I looked at Michelle. She said, "If she wants to see, then let her. You've already explained to her what was going to be done to you."

"Come with me, sweetie. I'll show you my surgery," I said. We went into my bedroom. I took off my robe and threw it across the office chair. I pulled down my PJ bottoms. "You can look but don't touch."

She didn't touch me but she held up her tiny index finger, pointed to each incision and counted to five. "What's that pink stuff on your cuts?"

"It's glue. It'll melt and fall off. And I have stitches on the inside, but they'll melt and I'll never see them."

"Do you hurt?"

"No. I don't hurt, and soon I'll be well and we can play."

"Yay! I've missed playing with you. Are you going to sleep all the time until you get well?"

"I might take a nap or two, but I won't sleep as much as I used to. Every day, Nana will sleep less and I'll play with you more." I hugged her. "I'm a little tired right now. I need a nap. When I get up I'll play cards with you."

She ran out of the room and slammed the door.

My heart cried, but I understood. The worst was behind me. I lay down in my comfortable bed and thanked God for bringing me through the surgery, and pain free.

I slept two hours. When I woke up, Michelle told me that Nameless had brought my prescriptions and my sister, Linda had brought me a big bowl of white beans and a pan of cornbread. I was hungry and I ate with gusto. White beans and cornbread was my favorite meal.

After I ate, I said, "Olivia, Nana is ready to play cards. Bring the deck and tray to my bedroom and we'll sit in the recliner and play. We played two games of War, we colored pictures, and we played a game of Tic-Tac-Toe.

After we played, I told Michelle I wanted to see if I could make one or two trips up and down the basement steps. "Are you sure?" she asked, and I saw a look of concern in her eyes.

"Yes, honey. I can't sit and lie all the time. I have to spend energy in order to build energy."

"Okay. But we're going to do it like we did before. I go down in front of you and I come back up behind you. Olivia can stand on the top step and count for you. She'll think it's a game."

I made it down the ten steps with no problem. I struggled as I came back up, but I made it and I was proud of myself. I seemed to be gaining strength by the hour. Olivia yelled, "One," when I made it to the top step.

"I think that's all Nana is going to do tonight. But tomorrow I'll make it up and down two times."

She clapped her hands and my heart melted. Olivia was still my fuel.

At eight o'clock, Michelle gave Olivia a bath, helped her brush her teeth, and had her ready for bed. They came into my bedroom and Olivia kissed me goodnight and told me it was okay if I lay down in bed and closed my eyes. I kissed her goodnight, and tears welled as I watched her hurry out of my room.

By ten o'clock, Michelle said, "It's time to take your shot. I'll get a syringe out of the sample pack they gave you at the hospital."

"Hand me an alcohol swab and I'll clean the place where you need to pinch up my skin. Then take off the cap over the needle and I'll do the rest."

We did the procedure with no trouble. Michelle said, "It was hard to pinch up a half inch of skin. You don't have that much."

"I know. I'm a bag of bones with little skin stretched over my bones. But we did it. Be sure you put the used syringe in a plastic bottle."

"Done."

"My two hour nap revived me and I'm not sleepy, but I need to go on to bed. I know you're tired. I'll take a diazepam and I'll be out soon."

I took an ibuprofen and a diazepam and Michelle turned out my lamp. I started praying, but I didn't make it to amen.

Chapter Twenty-Seven

The next night I woke up at midnight. My right pajama sleeve was wet. I felt the top of my pajamas and it was also wet. I turned on the lamp, pulled down my pajama bottom and one incision was pouring yellow fluid. I remembered a nurse telling me it was possible that I would have drainage and it might be blood-tinged which was normal. However, if I saw bright red blood and it was more than a drop, I was supposed to go to the ER.

The fluid was yellow but I didn't see any blood, not even a tinge. Michelle had bought a box of 4x4 gauze pads and paper tape. I'm highly allergic to adhesive. I was struggling with taking off my pajamas because the incision was pouring fluid down my right side. I hated to bother Michelle, but I couldn't dress the incision and change pajamas by myself.

I picked up my cell and pressed her number. I heard one ring, then I heard her feet running to me. She opened my bedroom door and I could see the fright in her eyes. I said, "I'm okay, honey. My incision is draining, my pajamas are soaked and I need help. I'll pull down my bottoms and you place three gauze pads over the incision, then tape it. After we get the bandage on, I can change into a clean pair of pajamas by myself."

"Shit! I saw your name come up on my cell and it scared me half to death." She flipped on the ceiling light and the bandaging began. Then she helped me change my pajamas.

"I'll try not to scare you again. I was a bit overwhelmed and I didn't know what to do first. If it seeps through my bandage I think I can change it. My pajamas won't be wet."

"No. If you need a bandage change just call. I'll know what to expect next time."

By 2 a.m., the bandage was soaked, but my pajamas were fine. I managed to change it by myself, though it was a struggle. I had to use my forearm to hold the gauze while I tore off two pieces of tape. I taped my fingers a few times, but I got it done. I was determined not to wake up Michelle. My determination had already gotten me through a hard life and I wasn't about to give in.

The next night, diarrhea hit. I was changing my Depends and bandages as fast as I could. When it was bedtime, I took two diazepam pills. I have gone from wanting to sleep around the clock back to insomnia, which had plagued me for thirty years. Then I reached up and took a bottle of pills off the top of the chest of drawers. I needed two Lomotil pills to stop or at least slow down the diarrhea.

Just as I set the bottle back on top of the chest of drawers, Michelle walked into the room. "What are you doing?"

"I took two Lomotil pills. This diarrhea isn't slowing down."

"Oh, my God! You took two? That's Dilaudid! And you mixed it with diazepam!"

"Oh, I thought it was Lomotil," I said, then I remembered those pills were on my bedside table.

Michelle threw her hands over her face, dropped her body into the recliner and cried harder than I'd ever seen her cry in her life.

"Don't get hysterical. I'll drink a glass of warm salt water and it'll induce vomiting." I didn't measure the salt. I took the top off the shaker and dumped it into the water. Thirty minutes later I didn't vomit. Michelle was still crying.

I fixed a glass of warm baking soda water. Again, I didn't measure. I dumped the baking soda into the water. I waited thirty minutes. It didn't work. I tried poking the end on my toothbrush down my throat. I gagged, but I didn't vomit. Over an hour had passed and Michelle was frantic. I tried to assure her that I'd be okay, but she wasn't buying it. Through her hard sobs, she managed to say, "Call poison control!"

I called, but the lady I talked with couldn't find enough information in her computer, so she told me to go to the ER. She also said that she'd call the ER, explain what I had taken and they would be expecting me. I told Michelle what the lady said, but I didn't want to go. "I don't think I'm I any danger. I'm lucid, I'm walking around, and I'm not sleepy."

She yelled, "Put your coat on. We're going to the ER!"

"Yes, ma'am. Sir!"

We got into the car and Michelle backed out of the driveway. Tears were still rolling. I said, "I'm sorry, honey. It's not like I did it on purpose."

"Just shut up, Mom. Don't say another word!"

I didn't talk, but I couldn't figure out why she was mad. Then it dawned on me that she was so frightened, her fear had manifested into anger.

We reached the ER and I gave the lady at the front desk my name. Before I could say anything else, she picked up the phone and said, "The overdose is here." By the time she had the phone on the hook, a nurse rushed to my side, put her arm around my waist and hurried me down the hallway. Michelle followed.

When I reached the room, I felt diarrhea pouring out of me. I said, "I'm sorry, but I just filled my Depends. I've had diarrhea for two days. I don't have control of my bowels, and I don't feel it coming until it's too late."

"We'll worry about changing you after I get an IV going." She picked up my left arm.

"I don't have any veins. I'm taking chemo and I have a port."

"That's even better." She cleaned my port, flushed it and drew four vials of blood. After she had drawn my blood, she hooked me up to a monitor. My blood pressure was almost on stroke level. "Do you take medication for high blood pressure?" she asked.

"No. My blood pressure is always low. Three days ago it was excessively low and they kept me an extra night in the hospital. I have ovarian cancer and I had surgery. But I dumped a whole salt shaker of salt into a glass of warm water, hoping it would make me vomit. When that didn't work I dumped baking soda into warm water. I didn't measure either one. I just dumped."

"That would explain your high blood pressure. That was too much salt at one time. The baking soda might have contributed. And both of them will cause severe diarrhea."

Michelle said, "I fought like hell to keep you in the hospital because I didn't want to bring you home and watch you die. Now, you go and try to kill yourself!"

"Honey, I didn't do it on purpose. I don't know why you're so mad at me. But I tell you what, you go on home, get some rest and when I'm dismissed I'll call Nameless to come get me."

The nurse said, "She's going to be here for hours, and she could possibly be admitted. We've got to get her blood pressure down. We've got to stop the diarrhea. She's dehydrated and we'll be running several bags of fluid through her, plus we're doing a lot of blood work, and that takes time to get results from the lab. We'll call you when she's ready to go, or we'll call if she's admitted.

I looked at Michelle. "Please go home. I'll call Nameless when I'm ready. Calm down and get some rest."

"The nurse said she'd call me when you're ready. I'll be back to get you," Michelle said, and she left the room in a huff.

My heart hurt knowing she was scared and I knew she was exhausted. But my feelings were hurt by the way she was talking to me.

For four and a half hours two nurses changed the chuck pads they had put under me and pulled one end between my legs, making a diaper the best they could. Another nurse came into the room as the other two finished changing me and cleaned me.

I was exhausted. Using an old expression that I'd heard my mamaw use many times when she was sick or after a hard day's work, I said, "Somebody needs to take me out somewhere and shoot me."

The new nurse gave me a harsh look and said, "What did you say?"

I repeated it.

"That kind of talk will get you sent up to the psych ward. We take comments like that seriously!"

"It's just an old expression," I said.

"Expression or not, I take it seriously!" she said, as she narrowed her eyes.

"Look, you can take it any way you want to. I said it was an old expression, and let me tell you something else. I haven't fought like hell for my life the past six months, to want to be shot now! For the third time, it was an old expression!" I said, raising my voice.

She narrowed her eyes and glared at me. There's two things a person doesn't want to do when we're making eye contact. One is narrowing their eyes, and two is giving me an eye-roll.

She continued to glare and I was pissed. "Look, Nurse Ratched, if you think this cuckoo needs to be in the nut nest, then you send me right up there. The first time I shit all over the place, I'll be sent right back to you."

One of the other nurses said, "She's fine. We'll take care of her. You go on and help the other nurses."

Nurse Ratched gave me another glare. I glared back and said, "And another thing. I happen to know that you don't have the authority to send me anywhere. It takes a doctor's order. The doctor has been in here to see me and talk to me, twice. I don't think he's going to put me in the psych ward. But you do whatever you think you're powerful enough to do."

I knew my blood pressure was spiking, but I was furious. I'd been through enough, and I wasn't going to put up with an attitude which had no merit. At the age of seventy-six, I didn't allow anybody to talk down to me, or treat me as if I were a child. And I wondered if she knew who Nurse Ratched was.

The blood pressure medication had taken my blood pressure down. It was still high but not on danger level. The medication they were giving me had slowed down the diarrhea. By 5 a.m., the diarrhea had stopped. The ER doctor didn't think I needed to be admitted. The nurse called Michelle, and she was there to get me at 5:30. The nurse explained what had been done for me and to bring me back if the diarrhea started again and to make sure I kept drinking whatever I wanted so I would stay hydrated. "Pull your car to the entrance of the ER and I'll bring her out."

I didn't say a word. I sat down in a wheelchair and the nurse pushed me outside. I got into the car and said, "Take me to Nameless. I won't put anymore worry on you."

"We'll take about that later. Just be quiet for now."

I didn't say a word as we drove back home and I told myself that I wasn't going to speak to her for at least a week.

We made it back home and still no words had been spoken. I went to my bedroom and went to bed. I was exhausted. I knew my precious daughter was too. She had been up for almost twenty-four hours, and she only had an hour to sleep before she had to get Olivia ready for school. I lay in darkness and my tears flowed. Before I went to sleep, Michelle opened my door, turned on the lamp by my bed and handed me a bottle of Ginger Ale. "You need to stay hydrated," she said.

I said, "Thank you." She was still in a snit, but she loved me enough to make sure I had what I needed. I heard her and Olivia talking when it was time to get ready for school. As soon as Olivia was out the door, I fell asleep. I didn't wake up until eleven o'clock. I didn't hear a sound in the house. I hoped that Michelle was sleeping. I was as quiet as possible as I made my way into the kitchen and made scrambled eggs for breakfast.

The nurse had changed my bandage before I left the hospital, but it was soaked, again. I managed to change it myself. I lay back down and dozed off. I awoke when I heard Michelle in the kitchen. I didn't dare bother her, but I was glad she had finally gotten some much needed sleep. It was twelve noon.

Michelle opened my door. "I made a fresh pot of coffee. Do you want a cup?"

"Coffee sounds good." She left the room and I smiled. She had lost her snit.

She came back with a cup of coffee, handed it to me and said, "You won't be taking anymore Dilaudid. By now they are at the bottom of the Ohio River."

I laughed. "That's a good place for them." I took a sip of coffee. "The sun is shining. Do you think it's too cold to sit outside?"

"We can give it a try. I miss our mornings being outside and drinking coffee."

The warm sun and the hot coffee helped, but the wind was cutting through my frail body. I lasted ten minutes. It was great to be outside if only for a few minutes and Michelle and I laughed about the day I had done a tap dance with a bumble bee. She rubbed the top of my head. "The anesthetic took what few strands of hair you had."

"Yep. I'm bald as a baby's butt. But since I don't have to take chemo anymore, it'll come back. I hope it comes back in red ringlets. However, I'll accept my snow white."

"Your snow white hair is beautiful."

We went back inside. We were okay with each other and my heart was full with love and happiness.

For the next five days, Michelle and I changed my bandage every hour. I couldn't believe that much fluid could come from a tiny incision. The diarrhea had stopped and I was glad for that relief more than anything else.

When Olivia was home from school, she helped take care of me. She pulled the paper tape, and I ripped it off the roll. She thought it was a game. It also amazed me how she took everything in stride. She never showed any fear when things had to be done for me. I often thought we had a nurse in the making. I hoped my thoughts were right. She would have probably tried to give me the shots every night if she had been awake when it was time for an injection.

Every day I was gaining strength. One week after my surgery, I was making three trips up and down the basement steps. I was taking showers by myself, and I could fix my own meals, mostly cereal and eggs. Michelle always cooked supper and I ate meat and vegetables. I knew God was pulling me onward, which was an answer to my prayers.

I also saw the tiredness in Michelle's eyes. She never complained, but my mother's heart knew I was wearing her out. It was the last thing I wanted. No mother wants to be a heavy load on her child.

Chapter Twenty-Eight

January 16ᵗʰ, 2019, was my seventh day post-op. Michelle and I had made the first trip down the basement steps. I said, "Sit down for a minute. I want to talk to you"

We sat down on the last step. "I think it's time for you to take me back to stay with Nameless for a while. You're worn out. I'm self-sufficient. If you'll help me pack my suitcases, I'll be fine with him."

"Mom, it's too soon. You know Nameless can't help you change your bandage, and you have to take the shots for another week. He can't help you do that either."

"Honey, I can change the bandage by myself. I've done it at night when you're asleep, and I've done it when you're busy. I've learned to use my forearm and both hands at the same time. As far as my shots, all he has to do is open the packets with the alcohol swabs, then take the tops off the syringes. Surely, he can do that. If not, I'll figure that out too. Now don't argue with me."

"If you want to go, then I'll take you. But if you have any problems or need help that he can't give you, I'm just a phone call away."

"That you are. Let's go pack." We packed my suitcases and I was a bit tired, but I was thankful that I had the strength to help my daughter.

She drove me back to Nameless and carried my suitcases inside. She unpacked and put everything in the drawers and closet. I sat it out. I was more tired than I realized. After she finished and went home, I went to bed. My big bed felt wonderful. Soon, I was sound asleep.

When I woke up, Michelle had sent me a message on Facebook: "Olivia came home from school and she ran to your bedroom. I was right behind her. She wanted to know where Nana was. I told her you were going to stay with Nameless for a while. She teared up, but I told her you'd be back soon. She kicked off her shoes and climbed into your bed. She said the pillow smelled like Nana. Within minutes she was sound asleep. While she was asleep, I took a shower. When I got out of the shower, I put on your robe that was hanging on the rack in the bathroom. When she woke up, she let me know I wasn't supposed to wear your robe because it smelled like you. She insisted that I take it off and put it back where you hung it. I guess she thought if I wore it, it would smell like me. I took it off."

I teared up. My sweet baby missed me and she wanted to sleep in my bed so she could smell my pillow. I chuckled about her telling her mother that she couldn't wear my robe. She wanted Nana's scent to stay on it and she didn't want her mother to stink it up. Olivia has always been a child who accepts things quickly. I hoped she would adjust to me being gone, fast. I couldn't stand the thought of her crying for me. If she cried after that day, Michelle didn't tell me.

That night I watched a movie on Netflix. I changed my bandage and I noticed the drainage was slowing down. I struggled with tearing off two pieces of tape from the roll, but I got the job done. Though I was using paper tape, it was eating up my skin. I had running sores around my incision. I wiped them with alcohol, which stung to the point it brought tears, but I gritted my teeth and withstood the pain.

When it was time for my injection, I told Name-less what to do. I won't go into detail out of respect, because he did the best he could. However, it would have been a comedy act if it had been a sitcom. I managed to get it done.

The next day, I was in a silly mood and since it had been several days since I had posted anything on Facebook, I decided I would make up a story and post. Most of my friends know that half of what I post is a joke and they appreciate a laugh.

Facebook post: I'm still too weak to stand alone in the shower, so I called several men and begged them to get in the shower with me, soap me up, rinse me off, then lotion my body. Not a single taker. I even told them to take out their contacts, take off their glasses, or just shut their eyes. I don't know what's wrong with people not wanting to help an ol' lady in need. Jeez. I need a shower. I stink.

Several people commented and said they were sorry that nobody would help me and they would be more than happy to help me if they lived close enough. Most of my friends commented and told me they were happy that I was back to my old crazy self.

Later that evening, Michelle called me and said, "Mom, I forgot that you have an appointment to see Doctor S's nurse, tomorrow. And you're supposed to go by the lab and get blood work done before you go to see her. I'll pick you up early so we'll have plenty of time."

"No, honey. You don't have to take me. Nameless will do it. It's too cold to play golf and he's not doing anything else."

"Okay. But do you remember the lab is four buildings down from Doctor S's office, and once you're in the building, you have a long way to walk before you get to the lab?"

"Yes, I remember. I can do it. You continue to rest and I'll call you when we get home."

The next day, Nameless took me. I was eight days post-op and I was still weak, but I knew I could do it. He took me to the front door of the building. I got out of the car and told him I'd be waiting in the lobby. It seemed like forever before he parked and came inside. "I've got a long way to walk, but I can make it," I said.

"Why don't you get in a wheelchair? There's plenty right here. I'll push you."

"I don't want a wheelchair. As long as the Good Lord lets me stand and allows me to put one foot in front of the other, I'll walk," I said. I was determined not to give in. It seemed to be a half mile before I reached the lab. I know that God was giving me the strength and He was pulling me all the way. I said a silent prayer of thanks.

I registered and waited for my name to be called. A male phlebotomist called my name. I entered the door where he was standing and said, "I came in my PJ's, robe, and house shoes so pardon my outfit. My stomach is too swollen to put on pants and my feet are too swollen to put on shoes. I'm bald and this turban makes me look like a dork. Do you think I stand a chance for the beauty contest?"

The guy was in his late twenties or early thirties, the best I could guess. He said, "I think you're beautiful. My vote will go to you."

I patted his arm and said, "Lie to me, baby. I love it."

We had a laugh. He said, "You keep that sense of humor and nothing will be too much for you."

Through it all I'd kept my humor. It got me through for sure.

Once we were in the draw room, I kicked off my house shoes. My feet were so swollen the house shoes were tight. "My toes look like link sausages," I said.

He looked at me feet. "Yep, those little piggies look like they ate a lot of roast beef."

"Well, none of them would stay home, they all went to the market, bought a roast beef and cried wee-wee-wee all the way back to my house shoes."

"I love your attitude, girl. Now, hold still and here's hoping I can find a vein. I'm not trained to use a port."

He had to use a vein on the back of both hands, but he got two vials of blood. "Good job," I said.

He gave me a hug, wished me well and said he would remember me in his prayers. I returned the hug and thanked him. As I left the lab I felt tears of joy wanting to spill. I was amazed by how many people who were praying for me. Most of them strangers, but they had the love of God in their hearts, and they touched me deeply.

I went to Doctor S's office. His nurse looked at my incisions. "They look good. You're healing well, and the drainage should stop soon. I'll change your bandage." She saw the running sores around the incision where the tape had eaten my skin. "That doesn't look good. Are you using paper tape? Usually the paper tape doesn't do this."

"I use paper tape, but I'm so allergic to anything that has sticky on it, I can't tolerate it. I've been using alcohol to clean it, but it isn't helping. Would it be okay to use Neosporin?"

"No. You can't use anything accept alcohol. Neosporin or anything else is too dangerous because it could get on the incision and cause an infection. You just have to tough it out. Do you have any more questions?"

"Yes. When can I see Doctor S and when will I get my biopsy report?"

"It takes up to three weeks to get biopsy results. Our office will call you and give you an appointment."

I thanked her and left the office. I'm not a patient person and I knew it was going to be a long two week wait. I hoped with all my heart since I was eight days post-op that I'd get a call within two weeks.

Facebook post: January 23rd, 2019. I want to take this opportunity to once more thank all the prayer warriors for praying for me as I went through chemo. I hope we're not wearing God out. Sometimes I think God is saying, "I heard you the first time. I'm working on it." But He is going to keep hearing from me. I'll pray every day for the rest of my life that the cancer will never return. The fear never leaves you. Tomorrow I'll be two weeks post-op. I'm gaining strength every day, and my strength comes from God.

As I waited it out, the devil kept messing with my head with negative thoughts. One day I was alone. I looked out the front window and said, "Oh, devil, how you love to mess with me. You think you can break me down, but I've got news for you. You might bend me but you'll never break me! Don't fool with me, you MF'er!"

Note from my journal: January 20th, 2019. I hate to hear somebody say, "If I can do it, anybody can do it." Everybody is different and nothing works for all. In my novel about my journey with cancer, the reader will never read 'It worked for me, it will work for you', because it won't. I will merely tell about the tools that did work for me. I might suggest the reader try them, then it's up to them. Some may even pooh-pooh many things. That's okay too. It will be about *my* battle, not the reader's. Hopefully it will inspire readers. That's my intention. My story is *not* about how to beat cancer. If I had the answers, I'd cure the world. Cancer is mortal hell, but it can be beaten. I will beat it!

The next day, Olivia came for a visit while Michelle ran errands. She loves to sit beside me as I read posts on Facebook, then I let her hit the emojies: Like, Love, HaHa, and so forth. Sometimes she wanted to click on one and I'd say, "No, don't hit anything because it doesn't pertain to me."

After we played on Facebook, I told her to get my purse so I could get the fingernail scissors. Her nails really needed cutting.

She said, "I don't think that pertains to me."

After a few minutes of serious discussion, she decided it *did* pertain to her. We got the job done. As I've said many times, Olivia is the fuel that keeps my fighting spirit aflame.

Chapter Twenty-Nine

As the days passed, I couldn't believe how fast I was gaining strength. I would be three weeks post-op in three days. I was making eighty-five laps per day through the house. One day, after I walked the laps, I cooked supper, took a shower, and made five more laps around the circle. My fighting spirit wasn't going to slow down, let alone stop. It was onward and upward with each new day.

Facebook post: It's so cold I'm wearing my turbans and sock caps inside the house. I told Olivia a few months ago that when the back of my head was bald enough she could take a marker and draw a smiley face on it. She's been anxious to do it. So, I'm going to let her do it today when she comes for a visit. Tomorrow, when I go to the doctor for my post-op checkup, I'm going to lay face down on the table. I haven't messed with Doctor S's head like I used to do with Dr. M. This should be fun.

The next morning, I was happy and anxious to get the results of my biopsy. I was strong enough to drive myself, but Nameless insisted, so I let him take me. We were in the waiting room for two hours. I was about to cancel my appointment and reschedule. My butt and back weren't going to be able to stand much more in the uncomfortable chair.

I looked over at Nameless, who was playing Solitaire on his cell phone, oblivious to everything around him. I said, "I'm going to give it thirty more minutes. If I'm not called back, then we're out of here!"

"Whatever you say," he replied, and I knew he hadn't heard a word I had said.

"I think I'm going to go outside and eat worms and die!"

He looked at me and said, "Huh?"

"Never mind." By this time I was getting pissed. Just as I got out of my chair to cancel my appointment, a nurse called my name. I wondered if Nameless would notice I was gone.

The nurse checked my vitals. Everything was fine. She had me pull down the top of my pants and she checked my incisions. "They look fine. The glue has about fallen off. Be sure you don't pull on it. Let it fall off on its own".

I asked if my biopsy report was back.

"Yes, it is. Doctor S will go over it with you. He'll be in to see you in a few minutes." She left the room.

It was another thirty minutes before Doctor S and his nurse came into the exam room. Doctor S walked in with a big smile, shook my hand and said, "My nurse said your incisions are healing and they looked good." He looked down for a few seconds, then said,

"The biopsy showed that both ovaries were cancerous, so were both fallopian tubes. There are cancer cells in the lymph nodes in your abdominal cavity. You need more chemo. I'll refer you back to Doctor M, and he'll work out a plan for you."

I felt as if I had been chopped off at the knees. Surely, he had the wrong information. I couldn't still have cancer. My PET scan had shown all clear. My mind wanted to travel off and go to a place where cancer doesn't exist, but I made myself stay with reality.

He said, "I'm sorry to give you bad news. I wish you well, and God bless." Out the door he went.

I didn't realize I was crying until I felt tears running down my face. I was too stunned to wipe them off. I just let them roll and drop onto my sweater. The nurse scooted her stool over to me. She held my hand and said, "With your kind of cancer this is how it always goes. You take chemo, then you have surgery, then you have to take maintenance chemo."

I still couldn't talk. My brain was trying to travel off, but I knew I couldn't let it. I had to stay with reality. I had to let my mind absorb what the nurse was telling me. I regained my composure. "I sure wasn't expecting this kind of news, but it is what it is. I'll deal with it and fight like a tiger to beat it."

She squeezed my hands. "Stay positive. That's the best treatment there is. Never give up."

"I'll never give in. The devil won't win this battle. I will!"

She patted my hand. "Would you be willing to do DNA genetic testing? You might be eligible for a trial medication and treatment. The testing can help you and also help others. It's used in research. It will also tell us if your daughters are at risk for ovarian cancer."

"Sure. I have nothing to lose and maybe a lot to gain. I'll be a guinea pig. And I'd like to know if my daughters are high risk. What do I have to do?"

"You'll come back to this office, meet with a lady and she'll ask questions about your family as far back as you can remember. It's important to know if any of your family members have had cancer and what kind. Then a nurse will draw blood. Your blood sample along with your answers will be sent to California to a research lab. It takes about a week to get the results back. When she gets the results, she'll call you for an appointment and she'll go over everything with you. A lady at the front desk will schedule an appointment for you."

I barely remember leaving the exam room. I felt as if I were wading in quicksand as I made my way to the front desk. A lady made an appointment for me. She handed me a card with a time and date on it. I was trembling and it was all I could do to put the card in my purse. My mind was still bouncing back and forth from reality to disbelief.

Nameless looked up when I came back to the waiting room. I walked out into the hallway, my tears rolling again. He caught up with me. He saw my tears and didn't ask questions. He knew it was bad news, and he also knew I'd talk when I was ready. I don't remember the ride home.

I went to bed that night and prayed with all my soul for God to give me strength to do what I had to do to save my life. I was determined to fight. A warm glow surged through my body, as if God and the angels were telling me they were with me. I fell into a deep sleep, knowing that the heavenly host were going to fight with me and for me.

The next morning I woke up and I told myself there would be no sitting on the pity-pot. I'd laugh, joke, keep a positive attitude, and keep my fighting spirit until my last breath.

Each day I gained physical strength. My mental attitude stayed positive. I spent time with Olivia and we played games. My oldest daughter and granddaughters came by to see me as often as they could.

Snow was still coming down, but I enjoyed watching the flakes fall and cover the ground. I never thought about cancer. I pushed it to the back of my mind and waited for appointments for genetic testing and to see Doctor M. Nothing was going to put a damper on my spirit.

I added more laps every day until I was able to do one hundred. I didn't do them all at once. I did them twenty-five at a time. I told my Facebook friends when I reached one hundred laps that I'd go outside and climb the swing frame. I lied. It was too cold for my old bones.

One day I took a shower and it felt wonderful and I felt more like myself than I had in months. I decided I'd put on makeup. I was attempting to put on mascara. I noticed that only two or three lashes were being covered. I thought it was strange because I knew the mascara wasn't that old and I hadn't had it long enough for it to dry up. I took a closer look in the mirror. I only had two or three lashes. I had no idea my eyelashes had fallen out.

"Bald and eyelash-less! Oh, well, by this time next year I'll have a head full of new hair and lashes. It gives me something to look forward to," I said to my reflection.

As the days rolled on by I was gaining strength, I felt good, and I was doing anything I wanted to do. If I hadn't known that I had cancer, I wouldn't have known. I was enjoying being able to cook, and I've never liked cooking.

Facebook post: "February 2nd, 2019. The doctors say they don't have a cure for my type of cancer. But I do. I'm going to flat ass will it away. My willpower is strong and so is my spirit. I so appreciate all the comments on my posts, the prayers, and the stories about others who were told there was no hope, but years later they are still here. This will be my story in a few years. The love and support from all my wonderful friends and family serves to give me more strength and the fuel to keep me fighting and refusing to be beaten by the beast, Cancer. I will win!"

Chapter Thirty

Olivia came for an hour visit while her mother ran errands. We were playing with her doll hospital. She placed Lucy, the doll's name, on a gurney. "Lucy has to have surgery," she said, as she placed the gurney in the elevator, cranked it to the top, opened the door and took her out.

"What kind of surgery is Lucy having?" I asked.

"Lucy's gettin' the same kind you had."

"What kind did I have?"

"The doctor cut your stomach open in five places. He took out your o-varies, your tube-alls, your ped-dex, and the basket that was holdin' 'em."

"Did I cry?"

"No. The doctor gave you medicine to make you sleep, and you didn't know nothin' for three days."

"How am I doing now?"

"Pretty good. You still got stitches but they gonna melt. When they done meltin', you're gonna feel good and we gonna play all day. And you won't sleep all time."

"You're right about everything," I said.

"I know. I'm smart."

The kid cracks me up. Once she's told something, she doesn't forget. After she went home I searched my purse for my appointment card for my genetic testing. I found it and saw that it was for the next day. I was anxious to get it done, hoping I'd qualify for any trial treatment. If I did, I prayed that it would be the magic potion that would kill the cancer cells.

The next morning I readied myself. I dressed in regular clothes. I put on my bra, which was slightly padded, but I'd lost so much weight, the top of the bra sunk in. I put water pads under my breasts and it filled the top of the bra cup.

I drove myself to the doctor's office, and it was wonderful being able to drive again. I was in the waiting room, hoping I wouldn't have to sit for hours. I had to go to the restroom, which was down a long hallway from the waiting room. I took care of business, walked back to the office and just as I entered the waiting room, I dropped my purse. I bent down to pick it up and my water pad fell out of my bra, over the top of my V neck sweater, and hit the floor.

I grabbed it as quickly as I could, hoping nobody knew what it was. I didn't dare make eye contact with anybody. However, if I had heard a snicker, I would have reached inside my sweater and pulled out the other one and threw them in the trash can for all to see. Though nobody laughed, I couldn't hold back a giggle. I scanned the room. Two women had their heads tucked and I knew they were trying not to laugh. I entertain people even when I have no intention of doing so.

I was surprised at how much family history that I remembered. The lady was kind and I liked her. I watched her draw on paper something like a family tree diagram. It took an hour for her to write down all the information. Then she took me to another room for a blood draw. The lady who drew my blood wasn't qualified to use my port. She had to stick me three times before she got enough blood. I was glad when it was over, but I was hopeful.

I went out to the parking lot and slid under the steering wheel. A vision of my false titty falling out of the top of my sweater sent me into fits of laughter. I laughed all the way home.

That evening I actually enjoyed going into the kitchen and cooking supper. I didn't know if that meant I was getting better or sicker, since I hate to cook. I did give thanks that I had the strength to do it. For the rest of my life I'll give thanks for being able to do anything. I didn't think I'd hate doing anything, anymore. I knew I'd be thankful to God that I was able to do it. However, shoveling snow will always be out of the question.

A week later, I got a phone call. I wasn't eligible for any trial medicine or treatment. My cancer was caused from a mutated gene. I was disappointed for me, but I was happy to hear the chances of my daughters inheriting the same kind of cancer were slim. I was undaunted. My faith didn't falter. I stood firm in my belief that God would heal me.

I had posted on Facebook many times about my battle with cancer and about my faith in God and Jesus. Many of my friends commented on how happy they were that I had found God and Jesus. Their comments didn't sit right with me. They were assuming I had found God and Jesus when I learned I had cancer. Nothing was further from the truth.

Facebook post: I'm going to respond to the comments and private messages, one more time, and I won't respond anymore. Many are saying that I've changed so much because I used to never post anything about God, Jesus, angels, miracles, etc. I haven't changed at all. I'm not the atheist in the foxhole who finds Jesus when mortar rounds are coming at them from all directions. I've always believed the same as I do now. But there was never a reason for me to post what God and all the heavenly hosts have done for me until now. I've told about that in three books that I've penned. God, Jesus, and all heavenly hosts have pulled me through so much in the past eight months, I wanted to share my story, hoping I would inspire others who are fighting the same battle, or they have a loved one who is or has fought it.

I kept seeing posts on Facebook about how your children will fight over your money or whatever you have, but they won't fight over taking care of you when you're sick and dying. I'm happy to say, this was not my case. My daughters took care of me when I was so sick I couldn't even feed myself or crawl out of bed. My children know that I have no money or anything of value. They did it out of love. My son would have taken care of me just as my daughters have, but due to his unfortunate incarceration he wasn't able to.

As the days passed I grew stronger. I was driving my car, running errands and doing a little cleaning. The house was a pig sty according to my standards. Nameless couldn't have cared less.

One Sunday afternoon I drove the twenty mile trip to see Olivia. I had missed her so much. Michelle had brought her by to see me a few times and we had played games, but it wasn't the same as when I saw her every day. I'll never forget how she helped her mother take care of me when I could barely get out of bed. She'd go into the kitchen, fill my water glass or bring me a bottle of Ginger Ale. Her little voice still rang in my ears. "Here, Nana. You have to drink so you stay highdated." She had heard her mother tell me I had to stay hydrated and she was going to make sure that I did.

Olivia met me at the door that Sunday, and I could hear her yelling, "Nana! Nana is here!" My heart overflowed with happiness as she opened the door. She hugged me and said, "Are you too sick to play games with me?"

"No, honey, Nana is getting better every day. We'll play whatever you want."

"We played board games and cards. She loves card games. No matter how hard I tried to cheat, she caught me every time. We'd laugh and she'd call me Cheater-Cheater-Pumpkin-Eater."

Later that afternoon, Julia paid us a surprise visit. It was so good to see her as I seldom do because of her work schedule. We had a long conversation and she told me about the patients that she took care of. She only told about the funny ones. All of us were in my bedroom where I had spent many days and nights in bed and in the recliner. She only had a couple hours to visit, but it was a blessed visit for me. Before she left I asked her if she and Michelle would lay hands on me and pray for me.

I lay down on the bed, and they placed their hands on my stomach and were praying, silently. Olivia walked up between them, placed her tiny hand on my stomach and said, "God and angels, surround Nana, heal her, protect her and keep her safe and sound. Amen."

Tears rolled out of me because her little hand and her sweet prayer touched me to the essence of my being. When she saw me wiping tears she said, "I'm sorry, Nana. I didn't mean to make you sad. I just wanted to pray for you."

I gathered her in my arms and said, "Nana isn't crying because I'm sad, I'm crying because I'm happy. Tears come for a lot of reasons. We cry when we're sad. We cry when we're happy, and sometimes we cry when we laugh real hard. These are tears of joy because your prayer made me happy."

"Well, okay then," she answered. More tears rolled as I watched her run out of the room. I knew she was going to get a card deck and the games would begin. Her Nana was well and not the sick Nana she had known for months. I silently prayed that I would stay well and be able to play with her and she'd never have to witness me lying in bed too weak to hold my head up. I prayed with all my soul that those days were over.

Chapter Thirty-One

My Facebook friends are the very best. One of them sent me the book 'Curing Cancer with Carrots'. But they have to be juiced and I have to juice and drink two pounds a day. Another book was 'Curing Cancer with Kale'. Forget it. I didn't have enough vodka to get it down. I've read and studied all the books about curing cancer with diets. Some contradict the others which left me confused. So, I decided that I'd pick out the foods I liked and stay with them. I couldn't stand juiced vegetables. I ate foods that were high in alkaline. That seemed to be the only thing that all the books agreed on. Some said no sugar, which was no problem. I never was a sweet eater. All the books say no coffee. What? That alone would kill me.

The more I read the more confused I became. I began to wonder if people were writing these books because they knew cancer patients were desperate and they'd try anything. I had to wonder if it was a 'get rich' scheme and they would sell millions. I thought about writing a book on how to cure cancer with vodka, just to see how many people would fall for it. But my heart would never let me do it.

Many of my Facebook friends sent me recipes on how to fix kale and said I'd like it. I tried them all. I can't eat that stuff. If I sauté it in vodka, maybe. I did try juicing carrots, once. I couldn't get it down. I wanted to write the author and tell him where he could shove the carrot juice. And the kale.

For those who don't believe in chemo brain, I can testify that it is a real thing. I'm at the age where we all start forgetting, but not as badly as I was getting. My brain had wiped out so much. And it had wiped out good memories. I had to look at pictures to be able to recall certain things. The sad thing was it didn't wipe out the bad memories. One day I thought my chemo brain was getting better. I walked into the bathroom, and remembered why. My bladder was mad. I chuckled to myself.

Before I realized how quickly time was going by it was Valentine's Day. I've never been fond of Valentine's Day. I want my family to show me they love me every day, not just once a year. My heart overflowed with love that day as I counted my blessings. I had a clean bed, a clean bald head and a clean body. I had plenty to eat, and I received many phone calls and messages from family and friends. What more could I have wanted for Valentine's Day? Or any day? I was a happy camper.

Later that day I was watching the local news. My sides were splitting as the anchor man told a story about a local couple. A man asked his wife what she wanted for Valentine's Day. She said she wanted tulips. He was a bit hard of hearing. So she got a bucket of turnips. The anchor man showed the bucket of turnips, and there was a heart painted on the bucket. The man thought he'd done a good job. I couldn't stop laughing. The anchor man went on to say that his wife forgave him. Priceless.

Facebook post: February 15th, 2019. If I'm not asking too much, I'd love for any of my friends who had cancer, or a loved one who did, or even somebody you've heard about, who survived cancer when the doctors said there was no cure, no hope and was given a few weeks or months to live. If we share what I call miracle stories I believe we can help others who are fighting the cancer beast. We all need our spirits lifted when we receive that kind of prognosis, which is what I was given. I say bullshit. Our bodies react to our thoughts, and I'm going to keep positive thoughts and believe in complete healing until I take my last breath.

Ice and snow were covering the ground and I wasn't going out on the roads. I decided to write more in this manuscript. I finished two chapters, did a little cleaning and I was tired. Though I was stronger by the day, I still hadn't made it back to my energetic self. My mind wanted to do so much, but my body wouldn't cooperate. I laid down for a short nap. As usual, when I try to sleep my mind starts spinning and I remember things and start laughing. This day I was recalling something that happened a couple years before.

I was at K-Mart. There was a man a few feet from me. He was tattooed from head to toe, even a web tattoo on his face. I couldn't help but stare and wondered why anybody would look like that on purpose. He cast me a mean look and said, "What are you staring at, old lady?"

Now calling me an old lady doesn't sit well with me. I was about to spew obscenities, but I thought twice. I figured he'd get a kick out of me cussing him. I thought I'd mess with his head. So, I smiled and said, "I was just wondering if you'd let me tongue you."

He looked like a blue blaze as he ran away.

I don't think I've ever been so insulted. A freak didn't want me to slip him the tongue. The more I remembered that day the harder I laughed. I finally gave up on a nap and decided I'd write another chapter.

Note from my journal: February 18th, 2019. It's so precious and heartwarming when my grandchildren send me messages on Facebook and tell me how much they love me. Love will pull me through this horrible cancer. I don't care what the doctors say. I know a Higher Power. Love and faith are my only hopes. But I have plenty of both. Thank you, God, for pulling me through all I've been dealing with for the past eight months. I will win!

A week later I was in the bathroom. Most days I didn't have the nerve to look at myself in the mirror, but I looked that day. I yelled, "Hark! I see little nappies of hair coming through my bald head. I going to get my baby curls back. If I ever sprout chin hairs again, I'll be so happy I won't have the heart to grab the tweezers and pluck them out."

Nameless said, "What?"

"Nothing. I'm talking to myself." I kept feeling the top of my head. It was wonderful to feel my nappies. I hated the turbans and I was anxious to once again have hair. Every day after that I'd rub my head as if I thought the stimulation would hasten the growth. I was getting my strength back and making one hundred laps through three rooms. I was cooking and I was growing hair. I had no doubt that I would beat the cancer. And no doctor was going to tell me differently. I repeated to myself, "What is impossible for man is possible with God."

The many prayers that people were sending up for me gave me more hope by the day. A thought ran through my head— *all people are connected. No matter where on earth we are, we all see the same stars, moon, and sun.* I was connected to people I didn't even know and they were praying for me.

Note from my journal: February 18th, 2019. I saw a beautiful male robin on the swing frame today. I kept telling him, "Mother Nature is pulling a prank like she did last year. It's too early to help Mama Robin build a nest only to have her babies freeze."

Last April there were four newly hatched robins in a nest. A cold front came in and they all froze. I don't speak robin, so I'm sure he didn't understand. I just hope the same thing doesn't happen this year. I'm the crazy robin lady of the neighborhood.

Since my strength had returned I didn't require naps in the afternoon and I had gone back to insomnia. Every night when I went to bed my mind would spin and I'd recall things from years ago. I had taken a sleeping pill but before it kicked in my mind traveled back in time to when I was eight years old and my body cast had been removed and I was learning to walk again. I started laughing as the scene flashed through my mind.

I was living with Uncle Tubby and Aunt Loretta. Mamaw came for a visit and I was showing her how many steps I could take. I fell a few times and it hurt my feelings. I cried, but Mamaw said, "Learning to walk again is like everything else in life. It doesn't matter how many times you get knocked down, it's how many times you get back up that counts."

When Uncle Tubby came home from work, I was showing him how many steps I could make, and I told him I still fell from time to time, but Mamaw told me it didn't matter how many times I got knocked down, it was how many times I got knocked up that counted.

Uncle Tubby laughed so hard it sent him into a coughing spell. I couldn't figure out why he was laughing. I thought Mamaw had given me good advice.

The more I thought about it, the harder I laughed. The harder I laughed the more wide awake I became. I finally put in a Netflix movie and half way through it I fell asleep.

My post on Facebook: "February 19st, 2019. I make a lot of posts on Facebook about cancer. I don't do it because I'm sitting on the pity-pot. I post about my condition in hopes to help other women, and save them from going through what I have and I still am. I'm a believer and I'll never give up. If nothing else I hope my fighting spirit will inspire others."

ing. Take chemo. Take anti-hormone pills. You talk it over with your family and make a decision you are boss. I do what you want."

My mind wanted to travel on, but I let the words sink into reality. "I don't need to talk it over with my family. I'm making my decision now. This is my life and I—I don't want any more chemo." It almost hurt me to hear it said aloud. "Tell me how the pill works."

"The pill stops the positive drive from growth. The hormones it will slow down the growth of the tumors and helps them shrink. If al . . . ."

"How many years on I stay on this pills work?"

"Hard to say. Hope it will work. Sometimes two or three years maybe . . . side effects the bullets look a bit better till it and then getter."

"I'll try the pill," I said. "as I wasn't going to accept the chemo give years." I looked at him and, "what do you think?"

"I think it's worth a try. You'll also have to see me every month."

I let out a deep breath. "I'll write the pill prescription out right away."

"I put in prescription. You must appointment to come back in thirty days. I make you one first your next appointment." He stepped to the door, turned and said, "Bye."

He had given me goosebumps but I couldn't help but chuckle when he gave me one of his infamous

Chapter Thirty-Two

February 20th, 2019, I received a phone call from Doctor M's office. He wanted to see me the next day. I was able to drive myself, but Michelle insisted on taking me. She wanted to hear what he had to say and she knew I didn't always remember things.

The next day we were on our way. She hadn't taken me to Owensboro since November 30th. 2018. That was the day that Doctor M stopped chemo treatments. I had no intention of taking chemo again, though Doctor S and his nurse had told me I would have to take three more rounds, and possibly more.

We were there on time and I was called back to Doctor M's office in five minutes. Just as we were seated in front of his desk, he came into the room. I wasn't going to mess with his head, I was nervous and I knew I had to be serious.

He pulled his chair out and sat down. "I don't give patients false hope. You want truth. Right?"

"Yes, I do," I answered and my stomach tied in knots.

"I got biopsy report from Doctor S. The cancer can't be cured. It is in the lymphatic system, which means it can travel to any part of your body. Now, this is what we can do." He began to write on a piece of paper and he read it as he was writing. "Do nothing. Take chemo. Take anti-hormone pills. You talk it over with your family and make decision. You are boss. I do what you want."

My mind wanted to travel off, but I made myself stay with reality. "I don't need to talk it over with my family. I'm making my decision now. Time is not on my side. I don't want any more chemo. It almost killed me the first time around. Tell me how the pill works."

"The pill stops the pituitary gland from producing hormones. It will slow down the growth of tumors and hold them at bay. If it works."

"How many years can I expect if the pills work?"

"Hard to say. Hopefully you get three years. Five at best. Most common side effects are fatigue. Hot flashes. Muscle and bone ache."

"I'll take the pill," I said, but I wasn't going to accept three to five years. I looked at Michelle. "What do you think?"

"I think it's worth a try. You have to do something."

I looked at Doctor M. "I'll take the pill. Decision has been made."

"I call in prescription. You make appointment to come back in thirty days. Nurse be in and flush your port and draw blood." He started for the door, turned and said, "Bye."

He had given me grave news but I couldn't help but chuckle when he gave us one of his infamous *byes.* I was partially in denial. My brain couldn't absorb that I could possibly have only five years to live at best. I silently prayed, "Dear God, please give me more than five years. Help me kick the devil back to hell. I don't have the strength to do it by myself." Peace flowed through my body. I took the feeling that I was going to win the battle. God, Jesus and all the angels were going to pull me through it. I just had to keep believing. I promised God I would keep fighting.

The drive home was mostly in silence. From time to time I'd speak as thoughts ran through my mind. "God didn't send Olivia to me when I was past seventy, just to take me from her a short five years later. I've missed out on most of her fifth year, but I'm going to live to see her reach her teens." Another thought ran through my mind and I said, "My PET scan showed no signs of malignance back in December. I got my Christmas miracle. Now the devil has jumped in again. I beat that bastard once and I'll beat him again!"

"I have no doubt that you will. You aren't called the Come Back Kid for nothing."

"The Bible says if you have the faith of a mustard seed you can move mountains. I'm a bag of mustard seeds. I've moved many mountains in my life, and by God, I'll move Cancer Mountain. I might just blow the damn thing up!"

"Blow it, Mom. My money is on you!"

"You know how hardheaded I am. No doctor is going to tell me shit. I'll live every day as happy as I can. I'll keep a smile on my face, joy and love in my heart, and do all I can for others. I do believe in the Great Physician. I do believe in the power of healing prayers. I'll pray every day. I'll rebuke the devil every day, and I'll never stop believing that God can and will give me many more years. I'll ask all my prayers warriors on Facebook to continue to pray for me as I will continue to pray for them. Ten years from now I'll yell, 'See there, Satan, you MF'er, you didn't win.' It can happen."

"Yes, it can. The night the rosary was swinging back and forth, yet the shadow didn't move was God sending you a message. Maybe God and the angels were telling you that they were going to move your mountain into the sea."

"That sounds reasonable. I know it meant something. It was almost spooky. We've experienced so many unexplainable things, it was comforting. God was telling me not to be afraid."

I was silent for a few minutes, enjoying the beauty that surrounded me. Thoughts kept running through my mind and I felt anger. "Damn this cancer to hell! No doctor will tell me I can't be healed, and no doctor will tell me how long I have to live. I'll live as long as I will myself to through prayer and rebuking the devil. I'll never stop believing that God and Jesus will heal me and I'll live many more years. The prayers from so many of my friends and my name on many prayer lists in churches will also heal me. I'll do my best to always be an inspiration to others."

"You've said that already."

"Well, I just said it again. It bears repeating. It doesn't make sense that I can feel this good and my energy is almost back to where I was before I was diagnosed, yet my body is riddled with cancer." Deep sigh. "But as long as I feel good, then it's good enough for me."

Chapter Thirty-Three

For the next thirty days as I swallowed each pill I prayed it would hold the cancer at bay. I had a few hot flashes, but I'd had them for thirty years. They were no big deal except these were more intense. As for fatigue, I had none. I was energetic and doing anything I wanted to. I had no aching in my muscles or bones. After walking one hundred laps my calf muscles would tighten, but they felt fine after a five minute rest.

Facebook post: March 3rd, 2019. I just counted my new hair sprouts. I now have twenty-four. It's a-comin' back. I was going to post a picture of my bald head, but chickened out. After going through all I have in the past nine months, I've been stripped of all dignity, modesty, vanity, and all I have left is 'I don't give a shit'. But I must have a tad of 'give a shit' because I still can't bring myself to do it.

Facebook post: March 6th, 2019. It's coming up on one year this May since I began with symptoms of cancer. I'm still getting cards, sweet notes and flowers from Facebook friends. I feel the love. I need your prayers. I'm fighting like hell.

Facebook post: March 7th, 2019. How many idiots does it take to fill positions in bookkeeping? I got a medical bill a few months ago. I paid it. A month later I got the same bill again. I called and told the lady I had paid the bill, and I gave her the date and check number. She fiddle-farted on her computer for a minute. "Yes, that bill has been paid. Ignore it."

The next day, I got a check in the mail. I'd been reimbursed for the amount I'd paid. My insurance had paid it in full. Three months later, I get another bill for the same thing. I put the bill in file 13.

Note from my journal: March 7th, 2019. I savor every minute of every day and do my best to make every minute a happy one. I pray that I'm not going anytime soon, but every moment counts. When it's gone it won't come back. Whatever is waiting for me in the future, I'll find a blessing in the situation and be grateful.

Note from my journal: March 8th, 2019. Between writing chapters I take time out to do my one hundred laps. For the past few days they seem to be harder to do. My calves tighten up and my legs tremble. I just keep walking and saying, "You can do it. Push on, ol' gal. Don't give up." I think it's one of the side effects of the pill I'm on. It won't stop me. Nothing will stop me!

Note from my journal: March 9th, 2019. I thank God for my waking up to face another day. I sat out on the deck this morning, watching the birds and listening to their sweet chirping. My heart filled with happiness. God's creation is breathtaking. Cancer will never blind me to the beauty that surrounds me. Cancer is what has opened my eyes to beauty that I had always taken for granted. I count this as a blessing. I find blessings in being a cancer patient, as crazy as it might sound to anybody who reads my journal.

Facebook post: March 11th, 2019. My thirty days are up. I took my last pill yesterday. I have to make the forty mile trip to see my oncologist, get my port flushed and blood drawn. Not fun, but I'm grateful that I'm able to do it. It's a beautiful day and I'm going to enjoy it. I hope you find beauty in your day no matter what you have to do. Be thankful you're able to do it. Many people can't.

March 12th, 2019. I went to see my oncologist. He said I looked good, my color was good and he was happy to hear that I drove myself to come see him. His eyes lit up when I told him I walked one hundred laps a day.

"Your strength come back. That good. Your color good. I proud of you."

"I got my strength back and I look good because my daughter feeds me Kibbles and Bits."

"I no believe. I told you not lie to doctor."

"How do you know I'm lying?"

"I know lie when I hear. You lie. I no pay attention to you. Nurse will flush port and draw blood. I need to know what your CA-125 count is. We call you later with results. Bye".

His broken English always struck me funny and his quick 'Byes' as he leaves the room cracked me up. He was onto me, but I still messed with his head every chance I had.

The drive back home was beautiful. The trees were adorned with beautiful green leaves, and jonquils were in full bloom. I was anxious to see the redbud and dogwood trees when they bloomed.

I was a bit tired when I got home but a twenty minute rest was all I needed before I did my laps. I noticed that I had to push hard when I reached my first fifty, but push, I did. As I was walking I remembered Doctor M telling me when I was taking my first round of chemo, "Eat! Eat! Eat! Move! Move! Move!"

I said, "If I eat then move as much as you want me to I'll move off everything I eat."

He said, "No, you won't. Do what doctor say, and don't give me nonsense." He smiled, gave me a thumbs up and a quick 'bye'. He enjoyed my nonsense but he wasn't about to let me know. I laughed as I remembered his comeback when I told him my daughter was still feeding me Kibbles and Bits before

I finished my first rounds of chemo "That good. Tell her to put Gravy on it."

That afternoon at six o'clock my cell phone rang. I didn't recognize the number but I answered, "Hello."

"This be Joyce?"

"Yes," I said, recognizing his voice.

"This Doctor M. Your CA-125 count is one thousand, one hundred and fifty one. That not good. My nurse will call when she get you appointment for PET scan and you come see me next day."

I felt as if I had been kicked in the gut. My CA-125 count was a few numbers short from being as high as it was back in July, 2018. I was going in reverse. I managed to say, "Thank you for calling."

My world went dark.

Chapter Thirty-Four

I didn't mention anything to my children about the pill not working, nor did I tell them I was going to have a PET scan done. I was going to wait until I got the results and hear what Doctor M had in mind for me.

March 13th, 2019, I went for my PET scan. A nurse injected me with radioactive iodine and as I lay in the recliner for one hour waiting for the iodine to run through my body I tried to pray. I couldn't. Again, I felt as if God had turned His back on me. I wiped tears and reminded myself that God was still with me. The devil was my enemy. It was a long hour and my emotions were all over the place.

A tech came to get me. I dreaded the torture chamber, as I called it. I had to hold my arms over my head for thirty minutes as the machine went in and out. My arms trembled and ached and I kept praying for strength to hold on. Finally, the tech brought me out of the machine. It was done. I tried to raise my arms and put them to my sides, but I couldn't. The tech pulled them down for me. I felt as if my arms had been pulled out of socket.

A nurse came for me. She helped me get my arms through the sleeves of my lightweight jacket. I wondered if I would be able to drive. I made my way to the parking lot, unlocked the car door and slid under the steering wheel. "Please, God. Let my arms work and get me home."

To my delight I was able to maneuver the steering wheel and my arms didn't ache. I had to be NPO for the scan and I was starving. I decided I would go to the Cracker Barrel. I had a craving for biscuits and gravy. I didn't have to wait. The hostess seated me immediately. I hated to be seen in public, wearing a turban, but my hunger overrode my vanity.

The waitress brought me a glass of water and asked if I needed time to look over the menu. I said, "All I want is one biscuit and a bowl of gravy."

Within five minutes, she brought me two biscuits and a large bowl of gravy. I ate both biscuits and I emptied the bowl of gravy. I wondered how my stomach held it because for months I could only eat a few bites and my stomach refused anymore. I drained my glass of water and waited for my tab. The waitress didn't bring it. I saw her taking an order from a couple a few tables over. I motioned for her. She came over to me and I asked for my tab. She patted my arm and said, "There's no charge. You have a nice day."

I insisted that I pay, but she wouldn't give me a tab. I thanked her and she said, "You're welcome. God bless."

I'll never know why she wouldn't charge me, but I believe she was an earth angel recognizing a frail woman wearing a turban and she knew I was fighting cancer. I God blessed her and I was choking on tears. I've never been a crying woman, but I had become very emotional since I had been diagnosed with something I never thought would happen to me. I left her a nice tip and went to my car. I made the drive home, enjoying the beauty and I rebuked the devil all the way.

March 14th, 2019, I was on my way for my appointment with Doctor M. I was in the elevator with an elderly woman and someone I assumed was her daughter. I gave them a big smile and the elderly lady smiled as if she hadn't been smiled at in years. All of us went into the same office.

My stomach was tied in knots as I waited to be called back to Doctor M's office. The nurse called my name and as I stood I realized my legs were trembling. I told myself to pull it together. I made it to his office and sweat was pouring down my sides.

He came into his office and pulled out his desk chair. I tried to read his eyes, but they were blank. My instincts were telling me I wasn't going to receive good news. He laid the image of my PET scan in front of me. My eyes were not trained to read a scan but I could plainly see dots on my body image. My body had lit up like a Christmas tree when the PET scan was done.

He pointed to the dots and said, "Cancer is in lymph nodes in abdomen cavity. Cancer is in liver and four nodules in lungs. Your only hope is to take chemo."

Again, I felt as if I had been cut off at the knees. I wasn't surprised by the cancer being in my lymph nodes in my abdominal cavity. Doctor S had told me what my biopsy had showed. The fact it had gone to my liver and lungs was hard for me to accept. I kept thinking the scan had to be wrong. It was wrong back in December when it showed no malignant tumors. But that scan had been explained. My tumors had shrunk and they were too small to show up. I wish I had been told this before I was told I was in remission. To me it was the worst false hope any patient could be given.

As I continued to look at my body image, I knew it was right. I didn't tear up. I didn't fall apart. I knew I had to fight harder. I was not daunted. I didn't lose my faith. I didn't give up hope that I could win the battle. My fighting spirit didn't diminish. My faith increased. My hopes grew. My fighting spirit was more determined to fight.

I calmly said, "Doctor M., Chemo almost killed me when I took it the first time. You stopped my treatments. It was doing more harm than good. Is there anything else we can try?"

"No. Chemo is your only hope. This time I give you different kind. It's not as strong. And I'll put you on immunotherapy. I can't cure you. I try to give you longer to live. But you the boss. You don't want chemo. You don't take chemo. You talk over with family and let me know. "

"I don't have to talk it over with my family. Time isn't on my side. If chemo is my only hope, then chemo it'll be. And I'm going to tell you what I've told my children. You won't tell me I can't be cured. You won't give me a time frame on how long I have to live. I'm going to kick cancer's ass! I'll be a miracle story that you can tell your patients for years to come!"

He stood up and extended his hand. I shook it. He smiled and said, "I like attitude. You keep it. What you think is what you get. You fight and I fight with you." He gave me a thumbs-up. "Nurse be in and flush your port and draw blood. Bye." Out the door he went.

The nurse came in with a solemn look. I knew she was expecting to find me crying. I said, "I wasn't given good news but you won't see any tears from me. Tears won't change a thing. I'm going to kick cancer's ass! I just hope I can still get my leg up that high. I do well to kick the can nowadays."

She laughed. "I love your humor. You're an inspiration to me. I know you'll be an inspiration to others as well."

"That's my intention. I'm writing a book about my journey with cancer, hoping to inspire others. The secret is to never give in or give up."

"I'm glad you're writing it. You'll never know how many people that you'll touch. I'll buy the first copy."

I left the office and my fighting spirit soared. Cancer was not going to take me!

When I headed to the elevator the elderly lady and daughter who had gone into the office when I had, came out behind me. Before the elevator door opened I said, "We're going to have to stop meeting like this." They laughed.

We got into the elevator and I pushed the down button. I asked the elderly lady if she was a patient of Doctor M's. She said she was and we agreed that he was a great doctor. When we stepped out of the elevator, I patted the elderly lady on the back and said, "God bless you."

Tears sprang to her eyes. "God bless you, honey. Nobody has said that to me for a long time." Her statement brought tears to my eyes. Joy flooded through me. I knew I had touched her heart.

March 19th, 2019, I took my first round of chemo. Since Doctor M had added immunotherapy along with other bags of stuff, it was a six hour treatment. The nurses seemed to be happy to see me, though they weren't happy for the reason why. They were used to me joking and acting silly, so that day was no different. Nurse T flushed my port and drew my blood.

"T, you know you're my favorite nurse."

"I didn't know that."

"You should, because I tell all the nurses they're my favorite."

"I'm always the last to hear things. But you're my favorite patient. Of course, I tell all my patients the same thing."

"I won't tell the other patients if you won't tell the other nurses."

"Deal," she said, and we laughed.

Nurse T told me that I only had to take the immunotherapy every two weeks. My second treatment would be five hours. Then I'd have a week off before I had to take another round. Doctor M had ordered twelve rounds. I prayed that my old body would hold out.

As I watched the bags of chemo drip into my IV, I prayed with every drop I saw that it would eat the cancer cells as if it were a giant Pacman.

The six hour infusion was tough, but I was tougher. By the time I made the long drive back home the dang side effects had already hit. I had a headache from hell and my hands and legs were trembling. I said, "Screw you, cancer! I don't have the strength to do one hundred laps, but by golly I'm going to do fifty."

I managed to do fifty, and my legs were trembling so hard, I didn't think I would make it to my bedroom. I willed myself onward. I lay down in bed, exhausted, but I said, "Tomorrow, I'll do one hundred. Bet on it, devil. I've always been a stubborn little shit and I don't plan on stopping now."

The crucifix that hangs on the wall beside my bedroom door moved sideways approximately three inches. "That's right. You won't win, devil. God, Jesus, and thousands of angels surround me. They will always be with me."

I fell into a deep, peaceful sleep.

Chapter Thirty-Five

The following week I was in the waiting room at the cancer center, hoping my name would be called soon. I wanted my five hour treatment to begin. The receptionist said they were running behind, and I was antsy, but I took deep breaths and told myself to settle down. Other patients were as anxious as I was and their needs were as important as mine. Patience has never been my virtue.

A couple came in and the receptionist asked the man if he was there for an infusion. He said, "No, I finished mine nine years ago. I'm here with my wife."

My ears perked up. "Excuse me, sir. I don't mean to be nosey, but I heard you say you are nine years cancer-free."

He walked over to the chair next to me, sat down and picked up my hand. "You ask me anything you want because I love to share my story." He went on to say he had no signs or symptoms of cancer and was feeling great. One day he had a headache. He lay down and took a nap. When he woke up he had a large knot in a gland in his neck. He went to his doctor and after several tests, he was diagnosed with stage IV tongue cancer. He was given little hope. He took chemo. He had surgery. He took maintenance chemo.

"I've had nine great years cancer free."

"You're a miracle," I said.

Still holding my hand, he said, "You'll be a miracle, too. Keep the faith and I'll keep you in my prayers."

He touched me deeply, and I realized it was no accident that I had to wait longer than usual for my treatment. I was meant to hear his story.

Two days after my treatment I was able to make the long trip to see my son who is still in the hoosegow. I use this word because prison leaves a bitter taste on my tongue. It had been a year since I was able to make the trip. We got an extended visit. Instead of the usual fifteen minutes, we got thirty minutes. It was wonderful seeing his sweet face and smile. I had to look at him through a plate glass window and talk on a phone, but at least I got to see and hear him.

I pray that God will let me live long enough to hug him one more time.

A friend who knows the chaplain and other people in high rank called and talked to them. She explained the situation and asked if there was any way possible for me to be able to see my son in a private room. The request was denied. My mother's heart cried for my son. All I wanted was a hug.

I knew I had to pull on my sense of humor to get past the fact I wouldn't see my son until he was released. That afternoon, I took a shower. As I was dry-ing my body I could see my skinny self in the floor-length mirror. I laughed and said to my reflection. "When you were young, you always thought you'd look like Mamaw did when she was seventy-six and you would be fat and your boobs would rest on your kneecaps. You're not fat, but look where your boobs are. I don't think anybody would want your tit for a tat."

The next day I was out and about, sporting my wig. Three ladies told me I had beautiful hair. I said, "Thank you. I can take it off and let you wear it if you'd like."

Their eyes widened. "That's a wig? I would have never guessed."

It made me feel good. I'm like Dolly Parton. I look good in fake. And it cost a fortune.

Doctor M didn't come in to see me the following week when I took my chemo infusions. Some days he is too busy or he's in clinic most of the day. My last bag of chemo was almost empty and I saw him walking down the hall. I called out, "Dr. M. May I ask you a question?"

He backed up far enough to see me in bed. "Sure, what you want?"

"I was wondering how much danger I'll be in if I don't let the nurse put the Neulasta pump on me?"

"Why you not want Neulasta?"

"That stuff takes me to my knees. I feel horrible when I take it, but if you think it's necessary, then I will."

"You don't want it. You don't take it. I check blood work next week. I keep you happy." He gave me thumbs-up and a quick, "Bye." Off he went.

The Neulasta is used to keep my white blood count up. I looked at the nurse. "I sure hope I'm not making a mistake, but I have a family reunion in two days. I want to be able to go. If I take the Neulasta, I'll feel like crap and probably won't be able to make it. I'm taking a leap of faith, but this reunion means the world to me."

"If he thought you would be in danger I don't think he would have agreed to let you skip it."

"That's what I'm thinking," I answered.

Two days later I was able to attend the family reunion/baby shower. My fourteenth great-grandbaby was due in two weeks. I got to see several of my grandchildren that I seldom see because we're scattered hither and yon.

A few great-grandchildren were missing, but my heart overflowed with happiness as I looked around the room, and thought, *Dang, I started all this. If your old Nana hadn't gotten laid many years ago, not a one of you would be standing here.*

I tried to make a little speech, but I got choked up and didn't get to say all I wanted to. I did manage to get out the most important part. "I love all of you with all my heart. Please remember me and my love for you. And cherish the memories of the fun times we had, especially the silly things we did and the crazy things I did with you when you were little and you thought Nana was the greatest. I pray that God will let me stay a few more years and we can all be together at the same time—one more time."

I will cherish that day for the rest of my life. God truly blessed me.

The month of March marched on by. April arrived and the world was coming alive. April is my favorite month of the year. The long drive to take my chemo treatments was beautiful. Redbud and dogwood trees were in full bloom, and the tulips were blooming. Tulips are one of my favorite flowers.

The chemo treatment side effects were mild compared with the first round I had taken. The first three days after a treatment I had a bit of nausea but I had anti-nausea pills and they kept me from vomiting. My energy level was good and I was still walking one hundred laps a day. My main problem was forcing down two liters of water a day to flush the toxins from my body.

Note from my journal: April 7th, 2019. It's a rainy, dismal day. There was a time when a day like this would have sent me into depression. Not today. I see the beauty of the rain. All the robins are tweeting, and it's a beautiful sound. I'm getting ready to go visit my sunshine, Miss Olivia. I thank God that I'm still alive. When I got to my daughter's house, I had a great surprise. My granddaughter, Julia was there. She bought me a Dammit Cancer Doll.

The tag on it read: "Cancer, you can't get me down. I won't let you do it. I'm a survivor and won't let you win it. I'm going to rise above the pain and fear, victorious and wise. You're not welcome here. Dammit! Dammit! Dammit!"

I told her, "I love it, honey. I'm going to take it to the cancer center with me, and when my machine malfunctions, I'm going to beat it with the doll."

Olivia played with it for the rest of the afternoon, and we could hear her reading the tag and ending with a loud, "Dammit! Dammit! Dammit!" We couldn't say anything because she was reading what we had laughed at.

Note from my journal: April 11th, 2019. I had an interesting day at the cancer center. I didn't get a private room as usual. I had a roommate, which was fine. I realized the young man in the chair and the lady in the bed were foreigners, but I didn't know they couldn't speak a word of English.

A nurse came in and pushed a button on a laptop that was on the snack tray. She asked a question, and the man on the computer spoke in a foreign language. The young man, who I'm assuming was the son, answered in a foreign language. Then the man on the computer spoke English to the nurse. I realized he was a translator. I thought that was so cool. My nurse told me they were from Thailand.

My machine worked and I didn't have to beat it with my Dammit Cancer Doll. However, my room-mate's bag emptied and the beeper went off at the same time as my first bag of poison emptied and my beeper went off. A nurse came into the room and she looked back and forth and asked whose beeper was going off. I said, "Both, you need to call in the caval-ry." She's used to me and she ignored me. I couldn't pull off anything with the nurses because they'd been dealing with me for eight months. Dammit.

The lady and young man left before my infusions were finished. As they walked past the foot of my bed, heading for the door, they waved and smiled.

I waved, smiled and said, "God bless."

I didn't know if they understood, but the young man said, "God bless." I assumed he could under-stand and speak some English. Or he could have been repeating what I said. Either way we God blessed each other and that was all that mattered to me.

Victory Over the Mountain

She lasted eight years. Another reason why I kept saying that no doctor was going to tell me how long I had to live and I thought he healed. I continued to say, "I can and I will" be healed. Or if the Lord my treatment will get the cancer cells too lazy for about or ten years.

It will always be in my prayers and I believe they will be heard and answered. Whatever mind tells my body is how my body will react. The power of positive thinking works wonders. Life has given much to me.

...

Thursday June "April 15", 2014. I had the best month in Earth in Jan that I can't do more prayer and well make a turning my way. And I definitely worry I reached wherever that he is able to take care involved with how our lord prayed to as I start night in my prayed 5th day and fell sleep a that at night. Surely goodness and mercy will follow me through all the days of my life, I'm so blessed.

Two days later I made a trip to the Dollar General and I went through the line where my favorite lady works. I don't normally wig or wear hat I am, I just went with my hair out. She said, "I just happened to all your long red hair."

I said, "I just happened to lose the last three weeks bare. This is my cancer hair cut."

She teared up and asked for my name so she could put me on her prayer list.

Chapter Thirty-Six

I didn't think I was going to see Doctor M. I had twenty-five minutes left on my last bag of poison, when he came into my room. He said, "Tumor markers down. Chemo working. Bye" He started to leave, but I had to mess with his head. He's from India, and he doesn't believe in drinking alcohol of any kind for any reason or any time.

I said, "Hey, Doctor M. Is it okay if I drink a beer when I get home?"

He said, "You want beer. Drink up. Be happy. Bye."

Dammit, that didn't go as I was expecting. But I laughed.

I asked four nurses if it would be okay to drink a beer. They all said they didn't think a beer a day would hurt because it was in moderation. I didn't want one a day. One a week would do me. One nurse laughed and told me about her uncle. She said he came in on Friday, took his infusion, left the center and headed to the liquor store and bought a bottle of whiskey and polished it off that night. I asked her how long he lasted. She said, "Over five years."

Another nurse said they had a patient who drank a glass of wine a day and her doctor approved it. She was given two weeks to live when she started chemo.

She lasted eight years. Another reason why I kept saying that no doctor was going to tell me how long I had to live and I couldn't be healed. I continued to say "I can and I will be healed. Or at the least my treatments will put the cancer cells to sleep for another ten years."

It will always be my prayers and I believe they will be heard and answered. What my mind tells my body is how my body will react. The power of positive thinking works wonders. Life has proven this to me.

Facebook post: "April 15th, 2019. I have the best friends on Earth in Facebook Land. So many prayers and well wishes coming my way is overwhelming. Today, I received a prayer cloth in the mail. It had been anointed with holy oil and prayed over. I'll carry it in my pocket all day and I'll sleep with it at night. Surely goodness and mercy will follow me through all the days of my life. I'm so blessed."

Two days later I made a trip to the Dollar General, and I went through the line where my favorite lady works. I didn't put on my wig or wear a turban, I just went with my fuzz top. She said, "What happened to all your beautiful hair."

I said, "I was wearing a wig the last time I was in here. This is my chemo hair-do."

She teared up and asked for my name so she could put me on her prayer list.

I teared up when she said that. We were both blubbering old ladies for a minute. I appreciated her so much. So many people were praying for me. How could it not work? I knew I was going to get my miracle. I claimed it in Jesus's name.

April 18th, 2019, I had a triple dammit day at the cancer center. I was there on time, in a jolly mood, and I laughed and carried on with the nurses and Doctor M while I was in the prep room. My jolly slipped a bit when I was told there were no beds.

I was taken to a room with eight recliners in a semicircle. They were so close together I could reach out and touch the person next to me. The recliners are made for large people. I figured I needed to be six feet tall and weigh two hundred pounds in order to fit. My five feet and ninety pound body didn't fit. My butt fell between the crack of the seat and the back of the recliner.

My back went into spasms. I twisted and turned, raised it up, put it flat, but the spasms continued. If that wasn't misery enough, the lady next to me turned on her TV, full blast. She had on a news channel, all about Mueller and Trump. The last thing I wanted to hear. When I'm in severe pain, I get testy. After an hour of her flipping through channels to find the news reports I snapped. Before I realized what was about to come out of my mouth, I yelled, "Will you turn down that *beep beep* TV!"

She turned it down one notch and said, "I only watch news on TV. The rest is trash."

It was on the tip of my tongue to say, "Like I give a shit!" I stopped myself as the thought ran through my mind that she was fighting cancer too, and I knew what a battle it was. I swallowed my nasty words that wanted to spill and decided I'd give her an answer that would make her think I was a moron. "I only watch cartoons. They make me laugh and everything else to me is trash."

She gave me a look that plainly said she thought I was mentally challenged. She turned the TV off. I was happy when she was dismissed a few minutes later.

Mr. Grumpy came into the room and sat in the recliner she had been in. Every five minutes he yelled, "I can't get any sleep in here. The beepers keep going off. People are talking too loud. Nurses are in and out." On and on he went.

My jolly came back. I reached over and patted his arm. "I know what you mean. I'm trying to sleep, too. Maybe we'll be able to catch a cat nap before we leave. And I can't wait to get on Facebook and tell all my friends that I slept with a man at the cancer center."

Everybody in the room laughed. Grumpy didn't think I was funny and he huffed up. The more he huffed, the harder I laughed. The harder I laughed, the harder the others laughed. I couldn't resist the opportunity to mess with somebody's head. He was the perfect target.

As the hours passed, the room emptied and it was down to three patients. We talked and a lady who I assume was my age or thereabout, told her story. She had battled cancer for thirty years. She had lung cancer, took chemo, went into remission for five years, then the cancer returned. She took more chemo and went into remission again. Her treatments and remissions had continued until that day. She said, "I've kept the faith, my fighting spirit, and God keeps delivering. I've had a great thirty years."

I was speechless. She'll never know how much she inspired me. This woman was a bag of mustard seeds and she had been moving mountains for thirty years.

The other girl was twenty-eight. She had fought and beat breast cancer twelve years ago. After beating cancer she developed an immune deficiency that can't be cured. She said she comes in once a month and takes six-hour infusions. I told her I was so sorry. She smiled and said, "Life comes with complications. I accept my disease, take my treatments and I have a happy life with my husband and my son. God has blessed me, and I give thanks to Him every day."

Again, I was inspired beyond words. The older lady left and the young girl and I were alone. The chaplain came in. He and the young girl had gone to high school together. They talked and he laid hands on her and prayed for her. Then he walked over to me and asked if I'd like for him to pray for me.

"Of course. I appreciate all prayers," I said.

He knelt on the floor beside me, took my left hand in both of his and prayed. I could feel the warmth of God's love flow from him into me.

My dammit day had turned into a blessed day. I realized it was no accident that I had been put into that room. I was meant to be there and hear the older lady and the young girl's stories. I gave thanks for being put into the recliner room with back pain and all.

I had been at the center for five hours and thirty minutes. It was wonderful being able to stand up and walk around. The trips I had made down the long hallway to the restroom were difficult, but it was the only time I could get out of the recliner because of my IV pole and monitor.

When I left the center it was pouring rain. I was soaked by the time I reached my car. I went into hard shakes and I turned the heater on full blast. By the time I reached the Parkway, I had stopped shaking, but it was raining harder and I could barely see to drive. I wasn't going more than forty miles an hour because I was guessing where the road was. Eight semis almost blew me off the road as they passed me, throwing more rain on my windshield and completely blinding me.

I pounded the steering wheel and yelled, "Dammit! Dammit! Dammit!" Then I recalled the older lady and young girl's stories. I was ashamed that I was letting a rainstorm get to me. I thanked God for helping me drive when I had no idea where the road was at times, and I took my dammits back.

Chapter Thirty-Seven

Every time I lose faith in our young, I get a big surprise. I was at the gas station and I was looking for the buttons to push—pay inside—credit card—debit card, and so forth. My befuddled chemo brain wasn't working that day.

A young man, I'm assuming in his twenties, ran over to me. "Can I help you?" he asked.

I told him I was trying to find the button, Pay Inside.

He pointed to a tiny screen on the pump. It plainly read, "This pump is out of order." I have no idea why I didn't see it.

I thanked him, then moved my car to another pump. He came to my side, told me to stay in my car because he could see me shaking from the wind that was cutting through my frail body and it seemed determined to blow me all the way to Kansas.

He pushed the right button, then he filled my tank. He was so sweet. He renewed my faith. Again I was amazed by how God always puts the right person in your path at the right time.

I went inside and paid my bill. I didn't have on my wig or turban, but the cashier, probably in his twenties said, "God bless you. I'll pray for you." My bald head let him know that I was fighting cancer.

Again, my faith was renewed. God bless those sweet guys.

Facebook post: April 26th, 2019. I always thought that someday I'd turn into Mamaw and have to let the seams out of my pants. I'm turning into Papaw. I have to wear suspenders to hold up my pants. And I have his bald head, save for a few strands around the sides and bottom.

I can't afford a new wardrobe, so suspenders it will be. Bright red ones. Sometimes it takes a little ingenuity. My hip bones won't hold up my PJ's. So I lapped the elastic waistband a couple times and clipped one of Olivia's hair clips to it. Tada! It worked. Red suspenders really don't go with my Boo Boo Kitty jammies.

As I've said before, when you reach my age you reminisce a lot. Last night my mind wouldn't turn off and I remembered one of the things Mama used to tell me. When I was a child I'd stick out my tongue when I was mad. Mama would tell me that I was going to catch flies. I thought that would be funny. So, I ran around the rest of the day with my tongue out. I was so upset when I didn't catch any flies.

I could write a book about all the things I was told as a child. If I was told not to do it, that's exactly what I'd do. I remember standing in front of a mirror and crossing my eyes because Mamaw told me they would stick that way. They never did. Though they used scare tactics it's funny to remember them. It gives me a laugh.

Note from my journal: April 29th, 2019. So much happens when I go to the cancer center and I don't post it all on Facebook. I was in the waiting room and the receptionist and I were talking about how fast time goes by. I said, "It sure does. I look in the mirror and see an old lady where Miss Thang used to be."

She said, "You're still Miss Thang. You have an aura around you and you light up. Your inner beauty will never fade."

She touched me deeply. May my light shine for others until it's time for God to take me Home.

It is now the month of May. One year since I began with symptoms of cancer. It's been a long, hard year. I've got fifteen chemo treatments behind me. Seven more to go, and by God's grace and mercy, I will be healed. I'll never give up.

Before I wrap up my story I want to back up to mid-April

Olivia and I love to get our hands in the dirt. We dig and plant flowers and herbs, and we make mud pies. One day we were out in the yard and I said, "We need to pull the weeds out of the tulip bed."

She began to pull weeds, then suddenly, I saw her pull up a tulip with the bulb and roots still on it. I said, "Honey, pull the weeds around the flower. Don't pull up the flower, it'll kill it."

She said, "I'll plant it back in the ground, Nana, it'll be okay. It'll live and grow."

I watched her as she pushed the bulb back into the hole, raked the loose dirt with her hand and firmly patted the dirt until the tulip was standing upright.

I thought, *That flower is like me. I was once a beautiful bloom. Then cancer snatched me up by the roots.*

With the same faith as my grandchild, I know God will replant me and I will live, thrive and bloom again.

The Beginning

###

About the Author

After retiring from her career as a phlebotomist, Joy decided to pursue her passion for writing. She lives in Kentucky where she spoils her grandchildren and stalks newborn robins. She's the mother of three and the grandmother of seven.

She has penned ten fiction novels. Three of them: *Give Me Wings, Wings and Beyond,* and *Wings and Faith* form a trilogy; a seventy-three year journey that will give you chills and thrills.

Follow her on Facebook for live updates:
https://www.facebook.com/joy.redmond

Books by Joy Redmond

Children's
The Dreamer (2011)

Adult/YA
Anna's Visions (2012)
Stolen Lives (2013)
DarkHeart of Hampton House (2014)

Family Sins Collection
Finding Will Hennie (2014)
Sins of Sandy Slough (2017)
Sins of Silverman House (2018)

Wings Trilogy:
Give Me Wings (2013)
Wings and Beyond (2015)
Wings and Faith (2015)

Joy's books are available on Amazon.com in Kindle and paperback.

http://amazon.com/author/joyredmond